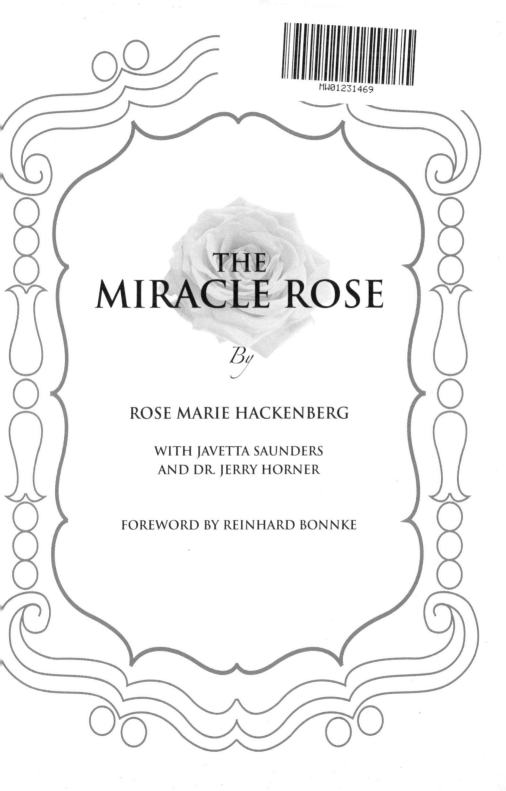

# THE
# MIRACLE ROSE

*By*

## ROSE MARIE HACKENBERG

### WITH JAVETTA SAUNDERS
### AND DR. JERRY HORNER

### FOREWORD BY REINHARD BONNKE

# MIRACLE ROSE

by ROSE MARIE STEPHENS
WITH JAVETTA SAUNDERS
AND DR. JERRY HORNER

FOREWORD BY REINHARD BONNKE

ISBN  978-0-88270-812-6

Bridge-Logos Publishers
17750 NW 115th Ave
Bldg. 22   Suite 220
Alachua, FL 32615

Printed in Malaysia by Akitiara Corporation Sdn Bhd

You may contact Rose at **rosemariehackenberg@yahoo.com**

# CONTENTS

# ENDORSEMENTS

This book is an inspiring testimony of God's saving grace. I am always amazed at the potential that God sees in individuals, even in those whom society dismisses as having nothing worthwhile to offer. Anyone who reads the contrast between Rose Hackenberg the sinner and Rose Hackenberg the saint can do nothing less than break forth in praise to God for His love and miracle-working power to transform lives.

**--Myles Munroe**

Rose Hackenberg is an inspiring example of how the love of God extends to all people, no matter how deep in sin they may be, and of how the grace of God renews the lives of those who trust in Christ. This book will give hope to those who are struggling with addictions and show them how they can be free in Christ. I praise God that He used the ministry of *The 700 Club* to bring salvation and healing to Rose.

**--Pat Robertson**

I first met Rose Hackenberg when we appeared together on Orlando's SuperChannel 55, and I was captivated by the thrilling story of how God delivered her out of the depths of degradation and transformed her character into the likeness of Jesus Christ. I have never heard anyone become more vibrant and enthusiastic when talking about Jesus than Rose, and her sincere and passionate love for Christ is transmitted in the pages of this book. If you want to be blessed and to bless others, read *The Miracle Rose* and then share it with as many people as you can.

--Donna Douglas, **Elly May Clampett** of *The Beverly Hillbillies*

Rarely have I heard a testimony that magnifies the grace of God as much as the one Rose Hackenberg shared during a live telecast from our studios in Orlando on a spring night in 1992. She gave an anointed and compelling description of how God made a new creation of her, bringing her out of the degradation of prostitution and alcoholism and healing her of liver cancer. Even before she finished, viewers began to call to request prayer or to give praise reports of deliverance from various addictions. The calls kept coming long after the program was over as people testified to receiving salvation and freedom from bondage. In this book Rose tells the same story of God's amazing grace, and it has the same anointing to point readers to Jesus Christ, where they can experience the same transformation as she did. I encourage you to read this book and then share it with those who need the life-changing message it presents.

**---Freeda Bowers, Co-founder and Vice President**

**SuperChannel 55, Orlando**

# FOREWORD

Jesus shocked religious leaders by befriending people whom they considered to be beyond the mercy of God and deserving only judgment. Jesus wanted the unwanted, and He offered forgiveness and new life to society's rejects. The gospel is not a word of judgment; it is glad news, not mad news. Jesus didn't come to "rub it in"; He came to "rub it out." This book shows the love of Jesus for the alienated and those morally down and out, and it testifies to the power of the gospel to change lives. The gospel apprehends us, stops us in our tracks, spins us round, and then gets us going in the right direction.

During my many years of ministry, I have witnessed thousands of undeniable and dramatic miracles, with no explanation other than the power of God. The miracles of physical healing are thrilling, and they cause us to praise God for His compassion and might. However, no miracle invokes praise and wonder and displays the love of God more than the miracle of the New Birth. Rose Hackenberg is a living miracle, because she is an old creature made new, a dead person made alive, a hopeless one enslaved by evil set free to walk in the liberty of righteousness. Reading this book will give you a greater appreciation for your personal salvation and it will cause you to marvel anew at God's redeeming love.

**---Reinhard Bonnke**

# INTRODUCTION

I first met Rose Hackenberg in August 1990, when my eleven-year-old daughter, Rachel, and I were in Los Angeles on a ministry trip. I had been in conversation with Rose only a few minutes when I realized that our meeting was most definitely a divine appointment. That realization was confirmed by the fact that Rachel and I were at the hotel where Rose worked only because a taxi driver brought us there instead of the hotel where I had a reservation. During the few days that we were in California, Rose and I quickly became close friends.

We also became strong prayer partners, and Rose has taught me more about praying the Word of God over needs than anyone else. I grew up in an Assembly of God church, and I always knew that the Word of God was powerful, but not in the way that she applied it. I had never experienced that power until I learned to apply it while praying. Psalm 103:20 declares that the angels hearken to the voice of God's Word and do it. I have stood on that and other Scriptures steadfastly through the years, and I have watched God perform His Word again and again in my favor.

I believe that, in addition to ministering to one another and to others, God's purpose in bringing Rose and me together is to write this book, which is finally accomplished after twenty-one years of friendship. You will have a greater appreciation for and understanding of God's grace after reading this book. To Him be the glory and the dominion forever and ever. Amen" (1 Peter 5:11).

**--Javetta Saunders**

8

# PREFACE

My name is Rose, and I am a miracle. It's a miracle for an ugly and poisonous weed to become a beautiful and fragrant flower. It's a miracle for cold ashes to become precious gold. It's a miracle for darkness to become light. It's a miracle for a living death to become eternal life. It's a miracle for emptiness to become fullness. It's a miracle for wretched hopelessness to become joyful expectation. It's a miracle for enslavement to degradation to become the freedom of righteousness. It's a miracle for a wilted Rose to become a flourishing Rose. God poured out His grace on an unworthy person like me and lifted me out of a pit of indescribable vileness and transformed me into the righteousness of Jesus Christ.

In this book I tell the story of how God brought me from the literal gates of death and hell into His Kingdom of life and righteousness. There are no adequate words sufficient enough to describe the misery and despair of my life before Jesus rescued me, and there are not words of praise sufficient enough to give God the glory that belongs to Him for saving me from that life. I do not know where God will take me in the future, nor what task He has for me, but I know for certain that my latter end will be greater than my former years (see Haggai 2:9) and that the years that I wasted will be restored to me (see Joel 2:25).

Some of the wonderful people that God has brought into my life to teach and bless me are in the pages of this book, but there are many others too numerous to list. They know, and God knows, who they are, and I express my fervent gratitude to each one of them. I especially thank Javetta Saunders, my priceless sister in Christ and the truest friend that any person could ever have, for her unwavering support of me. Without her encouragement, this book would still be only a desire in my heart. My gratitude also goes to Dr. Jerry Horner, who helped Javetta and me write this book. Mostly, I "give thanks to the Lord, for He is good! For His mercy endures forever" (Psalm 106:1).

# THE MIRACLE ROSE

I stood at the window of our plush room in the luxurious ski lodge, looking out upon the enchanted winter fairyland of Zürs, Austria. Robert and I had come here to spend the week between Christmas and New Year's Day for a few days of relaxation away from my exhausting schedule. I desperately needed a respite from practicing my profession, but more than that, I needed time to recuperate from the ordeal that I had experienced the previous day.

My profession was that of a high-priced prostitute in the notorious city of Konstanz, Germany, close to the Swiss border. On an average night I serviced as many as eight clients. In addition to being my lover, Robert was my pimp, and he controlled my earnings. In fact, he controlled my entire life. I was pregnant with his child—at least I had been until yesterday. I had no doubt that the child was his, because I always took special procedures to protect myself against pregnancy and disease when I was with my clients. When I finally shared the news of my condition with Robert after several fearful months, his reaction was exactly what I expected. I certainly didn't think that he would be overjoyed, or else I would have shared the news much earlier. Rather, I knew that he would strike out at me in furious anger, oblivious of the fact that he was just as responsible as I. In the bitter harangue that followed my announcement, he accused me of everything from carelessness to deliberately planning the pregnancy to entrap him and to "get off the game." He left no doubt about was to be done when he coldly declared, "We've got to get rid of it," and added, "I'll take care of it."

I knew exactly what he meant when he said that he would take care of the situation, and the price was 2,000 German marks, a little more than $500 at the current exchange rate. The person who took care of my pregnancy, illegally of course, was a mid-wife who showed up at my apartment a couple of days later. She probed at my slightly swollen belly and said, "You're in your third month, right?" It was more of an observation than a question, so I simply nodded, although I knew that I was much further along, possibly as much as five months. The mid-wife induced me with some kind of vile looking solution and told me that I would go into labor within six to eight hours. She assured me that I would experience very little discomfort and that I would abort the fetus with no problem.

Nothing happened after several hours, so Robert and I left for our Austrian vacation. Had I known what I was about to face, I would have headed for the nearest hospital instead of a ski lodge. The drive of approximately six hours was without incident, but as I was unpacking shortly after our arrival, I began to experience mild back pains. As I stood at the window admiring the pristine whiteness of the ski slopes reflecting the moonlight, I suddenly collapsed from what seemed like a massive blow to my lower back. Pain shot through my body and I screamed with fear. The pain subsided, only to return with renewed intensity a few minutes later. I was in labor, and the assurance of the mid-wife that I would experience no discomfort proved to be a wretchedly fabricated lie.

For the next seven exhausting hours I was crawling on the floor, crying and screaming in fear and torment. Robert had never witnessed anything resembling my suffering, and he thought I was dying, which was exactly what I thought. About 3:00 a.m. he was ready to call for a doctor to come, saying that he would explain that I had fallen and was having a miscarriage. At that moment my primary concern was an overpowering need to get to the bathroom. I could hardly stand, much less walk, so Robert helped me into the bathroom. I had just sat down on the stool when my insides gushed out in a torrent of blood and gore. Robert shouted for me not to look and quickly flushed the commode. After cleaning myself and soaking in a tub of hot water, I began to feel better--at least physically.

It was only later, just before I slept, that it occurred to me that my total concern had been for myself, without any regard for the life within me that I had terminated. I didn't even know if the baby was a boy or a girl. As I cried myself to sleep, I looked back upon my life and wondered how I got to this point.

    I grew up in a typical German Catholic household in Wemding, a small walled medieval town north of Munich, in the beautiful Donau-Ries district of Bavaria. I was the seventh child among a family of five girls and three boys. My mother was an extraordinarily gifted seamstress and baker. She was particularly creative in designing and making all our clothes. My only complaint was that the designs were not for individual outfits. The boys all wore identical clothing, as did the girls. In fact, on Sundays we were all the same. The boys wore white dress shorts and matching jackets, and the girls wore white frilly dresses. For winter clothing my mother would buy heavy woolen blankets and make fashionable warm outfits, including sweaters and coats. As a result of her industrious efforts, we enjoyed the reputation of being the best-dressed and cleanest family in our village.

    Mother was a devout Catholic, and there was no question that all the children attended Sunday services and went to parochial schools. Unlike her, my father wasn't much of a churchgoer, usually attending only on special occasions such as Christmas and Easter. While the rest of the family was in church, he was playing cards somewhere. Mother was particularly devoted to the Virgin Mary, and she made certain that we never missed praying the rosary every Saturday. She saw that each child faithfully attend catechism classes and receive confirmation, after which we were allowed to take communion, usually when we were in the third grade. The first communion was a time of festive celebration, and Mother was noted throughout the town for her special cake celebrating the occasion. There were seven Catholic churches in the town of 5,000, so she was kept mighty busy. She faithfully participated in pilgrimages and offered special prayers for her family. She would have been joyous if the boys all became priests. In fact, she arranged for my brother Freddie to enter a monastery to become a monk. There he learned bakery and later became the owner of a successful bakery. Needless to say, the boys did not fulfill Mother's aspirations for them.

In the early years of my parents' marriage, my dad traveled with a circus as an elephant trainer. He was away so much that my mother referred to him as "the Gypsy." Although it sounded exotic to me, she never approved of his transient lifestyle, so he found employment with the railroad company. His new position was great for the family, because one of the benefits was free travel for all of us on the train. We often took advantage of this privilege to visit relatives in other districts of Germany. My favorite trip was to the country home of my grandparents, my father's parents. It was another world for me, frolicking across the meadows, visiting the animals on the little farms in the area and gathering eggs in the afternoon. Dad loved gardening, and we always enjoyed fresh vegetables. He also raised rabbits, both to provide us with food and to sell. The only problem was that he would give each one a name and they were like pets to us. I never ate rabbit without a hesitant feeling of self-reproach, wondering if I were eating Peppi or Trude or Tati or Ettie or one of the other favorites.

Like many people, my most treasured childhood memory is that of Christmas. We always had a traditional German celebration, with the entire family gathered together. Our tree was a live tree decorated with little fresh apples, cotton balls symbolizing snow, candles on the branches, and gaily wrapped cookies and chocolates that Mother had made. Hanging from the ceiling was a beautiful advent wreath that she designed and made. It was decorated with red bows and four candles, one of which we lit each week in December.

On Christmas Eve Mother dressed the children in their finest outfits, as though we were going out to some special event. She had prepared a huge dinner, most always consisting of fresh carp, homemade potato salad, and at least seven other dishes. Dessert was a large pan of bread pudding topped with heavy cream, along with Mother's specially decorated cookies and candies. All of the children had special assignments during the busy days of preparation, but we carried them out with much joy and eager expectation, because we knew that *Christkindle*, the celebration of the Christ Child, was coming.

After dinner we would read the Christmas story from the Bible by turns and then sing Christmas carols. There were so many of us that we formed our own choir with all the harmony parts. My brother Peter played the violin and I played the flute. I have never heard such beautiful music since those memorable days. After the singing came the part that we were anticipating the most—opening the presents. Although we were blessed in many ways and never lacked for any necessity, we were not financially prosperous. However, in addition to the new clothes that Mother always made for us, we also received little gifts such as board games and books. One gift that I remember most vividly and cherished most dearly was a sewing basket that I received when I was about ten years old. To this day I cannot pick up a needle without thinking of those wonderful and treasured times.

As a child I knew my father as a kind man who worked hard to provide for his family as best as he could. Years later, after I was grown and my father had died, I was surprised and grieved at a revelation that my mother shared with us. She wanted us to know that our father was not the man we thought he was, so she told us about his philandering ways and the affairs in which he had been involved. I knew that he was gone from home a lot when I was growing up, but I never imagined that he led a double life. The most shocking revelation was the fact that my father had an affair with my mother's sister and they had a child together.

The most traumatic experience of my youth was a period of sexual abuse by someone very closely identified with our family, whom we trusted with our very lives. I was barely twelve years old when the sexual harassment began. For several months it consisted of inappropriate touching and suggestive remarks. I resisted every advance that he made and tried to avoid being alone with him. One day, however, he found me alone and raped me. Only a young girl who has been through such an experience can understand the emotional upheaval that it causes, with the resulting low self-esteem. Even though I felt thoroughly humiliated and ashamed, I could not share with anyone what happened, not just because of the turmoil it would create, but because no one would possibly believe that this man would be capable of such evil behavior. The abuse continued over the next few months, until he took a job in another city.

Mother was determined that each of her children would receive the best education possible. Contrary to the American system, in Germany there are only eight years of elementary and high school studies combined. I was an excellent student throughout my school years, and when I graduated from high school at the age of fourteen, I qualified to attend a business school. My sister Brigitte had graduated from the same school, St. Marie Stern Business School. I attended there for three years with an excellent academic record. However, I lost whatever interest I ever had in pursuing a business degree and I foolishly dropped out just before graduation.

It would be fruitless to attempt to explain my decision to quit school when graduation was in sight, wasting all that time and effort and money. Perhaps if I had received counseling after the sexual abuse to help me deal with the low image I had of myself, things might have been different. As it was, I just felt intense pressure and I didn't want to talk to anyone. When friends or family members tried to help me and to get me to reveal what was troubling me, I was afraid that if I began to respond the whole sordid story would pour out. I couldn't let that happen, because it would have been devastating to a lot of people. So I kept everything bottled up inside and spend most of my time alone. My emotions grew steadily worse until I felt such hopelessness and fear of the future that I despaired of life. I saw no reason to live; therefore, I did not want to live any longer. Suicidal thoughts began to dominate my mind. Death would put an end to all my feelings of failure and guilt and shame, and I plotted ways that I could bring it about. I could make it look like an accident to spare my family. It would be simple to walk in front of a car speeding down the road on a dark night. Many years later I came to the realization that my mother's prayers kept me from carrying out such diabolical plans. Thoughts of suicide continued until a little shred of hope broke through from my brother Freddie. At that time he was working in Switzerland, where job opportunities were much better than in Germany. He sent me Swiss newspapers containing want ads for jobs. Perhaps if I could just get away, I could leave behind the horrible memories that were haunting me and start a new life.

I had already disappointed my mother by dropping out of school and by my distant behavior. Now I would cause even greater disappointment by leaving home. But I felt that I had no choice except to leave if I were going to salvage what little dignity I had and to cover my shame. Mother reluctantly consented to my leaving only when I lied to her about my living accommodations in Zurich, Switzerland. I told her that I would be living in a boarding house for single workingwomen, operated by the Catholic Church and supervised by nuns. I involved Freddie in the lie by persuading him to verify my story. In truth, my brother had rented a one-room apartment for me that cost sixty Swiss francs a month, which at that time was about fifteen American dollars.

From the newspaper that Freddie had provided, I found an ad for an administrative assistant at a restaurant company. It sounded interesting, and I felt that I was qualified, so I secured an interview. It was my first attempt to get a job, and it was successful. I was hired at a salary of 500 francs a month, equivalent to 125 American dollars. To me, it was a stupendous sum of money that exceeded all my expectations. I soon found, however, that my newfound freedom had an expensive price tag, and it wasn't just money.

For a nineteen-year-old girl who had lived a sheltered life in a small German town, Zurich was a new world, and I quickly explored the depths of it. I soon became part of a group of partygoers and began to frequent the nightclub scene. In that group I met a professional dancer named Erma, and we became fast friends. This lifestyle, working by day and an endless round of parties at night, continued for the next six years.

At the age of twenty-five, I yielded to the desire to return to my home country, but after experiencing the delights of Zurich I had no intention of taking up a boring sedate lifestyle in my hometown. I would have spared myself much misery if I had gone back there.

My friend Erma and I settled in the university city of Konstanz, located on the Swiss border at the end of the Bodensee. Its history goes back to the Stone Age, and civilization arrived when the Romans founded a settlement there in AD 50. Actually, I wasn't all that interested in the city's history or cultural attractions. I wanted to taste the nightlife, and I didn't waste any time. Erma was dancing at one of the most elite nightclubs in the city, and I went to see her performance. During the evening I noticed that one of the club's hosts seemed to be staring at me. Every time I turned around, his eyes were on me. I certainly didn't mind, because he was quite handsome and I was very flattered. After engaging in visual flirtation for a while, we introduced ourselves to each other, and the vibes were so strong there was no doubt what was going to happen. In just a short while we declared our love for one another and I moved into his apartment.

Robert, my lover, used his connection at the club to get me added as a floor hostess, working from 9:00 p.m. until about 4:00 a.m. My primary responsibility was to promote the sale of champagne, the most expensive drink the club served. The cheapest bottle cost the equivalent of $200, and I used every devious trick imaginable to encourage patrons to buy even more costly bottles. I became very proficient at what I did, and before long I was bringing more revenue to the club than anyone else, at least through the selling of drinks. I had a way of manipulating individuals into hosting a group drinking party for other customers. I learned to spot the richest men and target them. My method was to prompt them to buy several drinks for themselves and me. I would pretend to be drinking along with them, while in fact I was pouring the drinks into a empty container. As a result, I was alert and sober while my drinking partner grew steadily more intoxicated. At the appropriate time I would play on his ego and suggest that he buy a round of drinks for all the tables. My looks and personality were very persuasive, and money flowed into the club's coffers as never before.

There were also some extra-curricular activities. One of the regular customers at the club was a wealthy man from Zurich, and he favored me as a hostess. One night he gave me a thousand Swiss francs and instructed me to take a train to Zurich and host one of his parties. Not long afterwards I accepted his offer and went to Zurich. He met me at the train station and took me to his palatial mansion, where he was throwing a big party that night. At some point during the party someone evidently put something in my drink, because the next morning I awakened to find myself in a strange bedroom. I had no recollection of what happened during the intervening hours. The owner of the house offered no explanation and called a cab to take me to the station.

Robert and I had been together for two years before I realized that I knew very little about his background. He never volunteered any information, and I was so much in love that I didn't care. One day during a drinking session he revealed that he was married and had two boys. I was enraged with jealously and terribly hurt that he had kept this secret from me. However, he assured me that he loved only me and convinced me that he had been separated from his wife long before he met me.

Whether he was engaging in false flattery to ingratiate himself to me or he was expressing his sincere feelings, Robert would tell me how fashionable and beautiful I was and that I was a high maintenance woman. As a matter of fact, at that time I weighed 120 pounds and had a fashion model's figure, which most men could not resist turning their head for another look. I loved stylish clothing, and I indulged myself with gorgeous outfits. During one conversation I shared with Robert that my dream had always been to own an expensive ladies boutique that would offer the latest fashions from Paris. I hastily added that it would take years to save enough money to fulfill such a dream.

A couple of days later, after commenting on my beauty, my elegant tastes, my business sense and my noble aspirations, Robert re-opened the conversation about the boutique. "Rose," he said, "we need to plan a business to secure our future. You're right; it would take far more money than we have now. You're doing very well at the club, but the kind of retail business that you want is still years away on our present income. However, I've got an idea that will get us the money in far less time."

I could hardly wait to hear his exciting idea for making big money, enough which would allow us to go into business. Before he revealed it, however, he built me up by describing the future we would have and enticing me with wonderful pictures of our prosperous social standing. Then he talked about how the city of Konstanz, since it was located on the border, was a lucrative market for prostitutes, drawing many men from Switzerland. This was not news to me, because with its nightclubs, casinos, and prostitution industry, Konstanz as well known throughout the area as Sin City. But I couldn't understand what the evils of the city had to do with Robert and me earning enough money to start a business.

Suddenly, by the way he was looking at me while he was talking, the reality of what he was suggesting staggered me worse than a kick in my teeth. I desperately wanted not to believe that the man that I loved and who professed to love me was willing for me to sell my body to men. More than that, he was actually suggesting that I become a professional prostitute. My church days may have been long behind me, but what little moral fortitude that remained in me recoiled in genuine and astonishing shock. They say that love blinds, and I guess it's a true saying. Robert soothingly convinced me that prostituting myself would be only a temporary necessity and the quickest way to get the funds we needed to start a business that would establish us for life. Because I loved and trusted him, I was oblivious to the sordid greed and total selfishness that would cause him to defile me for his own profit. I was completely under the control of this man, and I wanted so much to please him that I finally agreed to his abhorrent scheme.

Society may treat prostitution with titillating humor and Hollywood may glamorize it, as in the movie *Pretty Woman,* and the press may sensationalize it as it did in the case of Heidi Fleiss, but anything that presents prostitution in a positive way is a total myth. In reality, there is nothing more debasing to the dignity of womanhood. I know of nothing about the activities related to prostitution that in any way contributes to human dignity and worth. In fact, turning human intimacy into a commodity distorts an act that God designed as an expression of love and makes it a commercial transaction without a thought of the physical, social, emotional, mental and spiritual harm that it generates. Prostitution is intrinsically traumatizing, and most often leads to drug and alcohol dependence, humiliating and degrading acts, violence and physical danger, and health problems. A dehumanized woman contemplating suicide is far different from the "happy hooker" image that the world presents.

I did not know these things at the time, nor did I even contemplate them. It never occurred to me that Robert would be to me anything other than what he had been. I saw him as the love of my life, the inseparable one whom I would marry some day and with whom I would spend the rest of my life. I could not see him as a pimp who would control me to the extent that he would take the earnings I received from having sex with five to eight strangers every day and give me a pittance of an allowance. I would learn later that in prostitution the client performs the sex act with the prostitute, but subcontracts the intimidation and violence to another man, the pimp.

I knew nothing of soliciting men for paid sex, but evidently Robert knew the ropes. He introduced me to Ingrid, a beautiful young prostitute who would teach me all I needed to know about the business. My street education began the night I met her. I was no prude, and I thought I possessed a mature knowledge of the basic facts of life, but the things she told me about attracting and pleasing men blew me away. She also told me how to protect myself against disease and sadists who delighted to inflict pain on someone.

In later retrospect, I realized that Ingrid was the one who needed to be taught, because she had no understanding of life and had no concept of its value. In a casual matter-of-fact manner, she told me that she had experienced six abortions. I'll never forget her callous statement, "I have children like cats, but it doesn't harm me to abort them." This is how I learned about abortion as a birth-control method. I truly regret that I did not run away from this prospective lifestyle as far as I could after meeting Ingrid and seeing what it had done to her. Instead, we became close friends and she trained me as a seductress.

I learned my new profession very well and very quickly. I was young and attractive, and I dressed in alluring and provocative clothing to attract men. When I was working I customarily wore a tight mini-skirt and boots or stiletto heels. I used exotic make-up excessively, and I wore a wig with long black hair that gave me a "come hither" look. I averaged about ten customers every night, charging by the hour. My minimum fee was a hundred Deutsch marks per hour, but it was not uncommon for me to receive two or three times that amount. I would try to keep control of the time and manipulate the customer with conversation and a drink. I learned to feign passion and interest, while in reality I was strictly impersonal, having convinced myself that this was just a way to make a living.

Prostitution is very common in Europe, and there are many streetwalkers. I discovered that the competition was very fierce, particularly in the busy nightclub section of the city, and there was a great deal of jealousy from the older ladies toward the younger and more popular ones. I did not use many of the tricks of the trade common among prostitutes. For example, most of them used coarse vulgarity to arouse their clients, but I never used that kind of language when conversing with my customers.

I always tried to act like a normal lady from the neighborhood, which caused many of them to ask why I was involved in this kind of lifestyle. I gave the same answer every time: "Oh, this is just temporary. I want to own a boutique and this is the quickest way to make enough money to pay for it."

A year and a half after I met Ingrid, she committed suicide by overdosing on pills. She was only twenty-nine years old when she died. Her death should have been her greatest lesson to me, but unfortunately by that time I was beyond learning.

Ingrid wasn't my only acquaintance to experience a tragic death. There were many others, one of whom was Hilda. When a streetwalker picks up a stranger, she never knows the danger he may present. Some men are predators prowling the streets for victims from whom they can gain pleasure by inflicting upon her fear, pain and humiliation. They are sadists, using women in a ways that are bizarre, painful, disgusting and often fatal. Hilda had been a working girl for many years, and her instincts usually warned her about such perverts, but they failed her one night. The mildest, kindest and most courteous man could turn out to be the vilest and most cruel masochist, and one of them went with Hilda to the room where she did her entertaining. When no one saw her the next couple of nights, a friend went to her room, there to find her brutally mutilated body. She was bound in a horribly grotesque manner and her murderer had performed violent sadistic acts upon her before strangling her. As a final insult, he wrote the word "pig" on the mirror in her room.

I met my share of psychopaths as well, and I never knew what to expect on a given night. One of my most dreadful experiences occurred not long after I had been on the streets. I took a customer to my room, and as soon as I turned and saw the satanic expression on his face I knew I was in trouble. I stood frozen in horror, and before I could react with even a scream, his hands were gripping my throat in a strangulation hold. As I struggled for my life, certain that he was going to kill me, he hissed in my ear with an evil sneer: "Don't say a word and cooperate with everything I do, or I'll kill you!" After brutally and unspeakably violating my body, he took all my money and fled. I was paralyzed with fear and traumatism and lay motionless for a long time, whimpering with shock and pain. Finally, I soaked in a hot bath until I felt physically and emotionally restored.

On another occasion, about three o'clock in the morning, a man picked me up on the street. After he received my services, he drove me back to the same place, where I knew that Robert would soon meet me to take me home. As I was exiting the car, the man snatched at my purse, which contained hundreds of marks from my night's earnings. I held on with all my might and screamed as loudly as I could. A passerby came running to my rescue and the would-be robber made his getaway. Even though I was shaking with rage and fear, I was overcome with joy that I still had my purse with its contents. By this time I was thoroughly under Robert's control, and he took all my earnings. If I had nothing to give him, he would have been furious and would have vented his wrath on me.

I was living in such fear that for safety's sake, I secured a room in a place called the Eros Center. It was appropriately named, because it was a place where prostitutes carried out their trade. Not long after I began entertaining there, I serviced a soldier in the French army. He made certain demands of me to which I did not comply, but I tried to deceive him into thinking that I was doing just what he directed. However, he discovered my deception and became enraged. To my relief, he did not become physically violent against me, but as he stormed out of the room he vowed to get even with me, along with the entire center.

True to his word, the soldier carried out his threat a couple of nights later. He returned to the Eros Center and planted a bomb in the basement.

Unknown to him, I had left earlier than usual, but when the bomb detonated, many girls and their customers were seriously injured and the building was practically destroyed. The incident was headline news throughout Germany, especially because of the titillating report that it happened at a brothel. The forensic evidence gathered by the German police indicated that the bomb was of French origin, and further investigation revealed that such a bomb had been stolen from the nearby French military base. Internal investigation by the French military authorities led to the soldier whom I had serviced. To my dismay, I was taken to the base to identify the suspect. Because of my fear that the soldier would exact even further vengeance on me, I was hesitant to cooperate, but the authorities assured me that I would be behind a one-way glass window and the suspect would never know I was there. They put him in a line-up with several other soldiers of similar build, but there was no mistaking my identification.

This kind of lifestyle was taking a toll on my, and a spirit of fear and self-debasement came upon me. I began taking high doses of Valium and drinking a large volume of liquor every day. It was time for a change. Unfortunately, the change was not in the lifestyle but in the city where I lived it.

Robert and I moved to Ulm, Germany, best known as the birthplace of Albert Einstein and for having the church with the tallest steeple in the world, the magnificent Ulm Minster, or Ulmer Münster, as it is known in Germany. There we bought a luxurious two-bedroom condo, with my earnings of course. I didn't know it at the time, but I soon discovered that this was the city where Robert's wife and two sons lived.

Before our relocation, I had been practicing a low-class street prostitution. The only change in my lifestyle was that now I was engaged in the same business, only in a more exquisite fashion. Even though I felt safer, my fear remained and became even more intensified, with the result that I became more heavily involved in alcoholism, chain smoking and prescription drugs. Anyone who knew me before I took up this lifestyle would not believe that I could have plummeted so low in such a short while.

One night shortly after we moved to Ulm, I returned to the apartment with an excruciatingly painful toothache. I'll never know how I managed to smile and pretend that I was enjoying all my liaisons. I was near collapse, so I took a heavy dose of pain medication. It didn't touch the pain, so I got in a tub of hot water and proceeded to drink, on top of the medicine, a liter of red wine. I have no memory of anything after that until I woke up to find myself strapped in a bed in the psycho ward of a hospital. I had passed out in the tub, and I would have drowned had not Robert returned from a trip out of town a day earlier than he had planned. He found me in time and rushed me to the hospital.

The medical doctor had already attended to my physical condition, but the hospital would not release me until I had been cleared by a psychiatric examination. A psychiatrist began his interview by asking me why I wanted to kill myself. I explained that I had no intention of committing suicide. I had simply passed out from drinking a destructive concoction of pain medicine and wine in an attempt to find relief from an unbearable toothache. He didn't believe me until I insisted that he bring in a dentist to treat me. Only then was I released. That night I was back in business.

Ever since I had left the family home in Wemding for the easy life of Zurich, I had fed my mother a steady diet of lies about my activities. For the first few years, it wasn't so difficult to practice deceit. After all, I was engaged in a legitimate business  even though I knew Mother would not approve of my liberated morality. Deceit didn't come to easily after I began to prostitute myself. My mother always had a keen sensitivity, and her questions evidenced the fact that she had strong suspicions about my lifestyle and that my lies were no longer effective.

The last thing that I expected or wanted to happen took place while I was at my accustomed place on the street one night. A tearful voice from behind me spoke my name. Even if I had not recognized her voice, I would have known immediately that it was my mother, because she used her exclusive reference to me, "Rose Marie." By the way she spoke my name, it sounded like a question, a prayer and a plea all at the same time. My insides were gripped by a combined fear and shame that I had never experienced. She was behind me, so if I hurriedly walked away, perhaps she would think she was mistaken. I didn't turn around toward her. I shook my head as an indication that she had mistaken me for someone else and started hurrying away. She followed, and once again I heard the same plea, with a higher note of urgency—"Rose Marie!" As I ran toward my car, I could still hear her footsteps. The last thing I heard as I was closing the door of my car was a sobbing, "I love you."

I saw my mother's pleading face in the car mirror as I drove away. Embarrassment, shame and humiliation overwhelmed me, and pain pierced through my heart like a hot sword. How did she find me? It was only later that I discovered that Mother had gone on the streets, asking other working girls if they knew me and where I might be. Even now, years later, remembrance of this incident always brings to mind the story of the shepherd who left his 99 sheep and went after the one that was lost. That was what my mother did, but the ending wasn't the same happy result. I have lived with the regret that I didn't turn and bury myself in her embrace and go home with her.

34

The horrible abortion in Zürs that I described happened during Christmas of 1971. A couple of days after the ordeal, with lots of time sweating in the sauna and resting in bed, I was fit for the ski slope. That's a vacation I'll never forget!

Along with the other guests at the lodge, Robert and I celebrated New Years Eve in the bar, getting drunk on scotch and champagne. After midnight and the beginning of 1972, everyone was intoxicated enough to start taking liberties with total strangers. One man in particular was getting quite familiar with me and started pawing and kissing me. Robert turned from his own dalliance long enough to see what was going on. I was his private possession, and his territory was being invaded, so, drunk as he was, he grabbed the man by the collar and shoved him to the floor. The man retaliated by grabbing a heavy champagne bottle by the neck and smashing it into Robert's face with a mighty blow that knocked him into total oblivion. His face was pulverized, and through the spurting blood I could see that his nose was crushed into an unrecognizable mass of tissue and bone.

The alarming sight of my lover's disfigured face traumatized me to the extent that I was sober enough to scream for an ambulance. Medics soon arrived and rushed Robert to the hospital, where careful surgery corrected the damage to his nose. However, his recuperation required that we spend another two and a half weeks at the lodge. I was ecstatic, not at Robert's suffering, but because I didn't have to go back to my sordid lifestyle. Over the next few days at this lovely resort, I had the opportunity to feel like a normal woman again. I didn't have to walk the streets and assume another identity and pretend that I was enjoying fulfilling men's lustful fantasies. I rather liked becoming a nurse and taking care of Robert. It was a time of healing for both of us.

Unfortunately, we couldn't stay in this winter paradise forever, so all too soon we headed back to business as usual on the streets in Germany. During Robert's recuperation, we agreed that perhaps we should move to another city. I had already learned that in my profession it was good to rotate locations, because becoming a new face in a different area provided new opportunities to solicit clients. If that's true within a city, how much more would it be true in a different city altogether?

We decided to move to the much larger city of Munich, where there was a more prosperous lifestyle and my opportunities would be greater. We secured a lovely apartment, again with my earnings, and moved to the historic capital of Bavaria. I immediately began practicing my profession and was busier than ever. Robert did not have a job. Why should he work when he could take my money and be a man of leisure? He spent a lot of his time, or at least I thought he did, with his two boys, aged eight and ten.

Soon after my arrival in Munich, I became a close friend with Crystal, another working girl. We were naturally drawn to each other because our personalities were so similar and we could easily talk to each other. During lulls at night when neither of us was servicing a client, we had coffee together and shared our experiences and problems. We became such close confidantes that we felt that we could tell each other our deepest secrets and desires. Because of that relationship, I made some startling discoveries about the man that I loved and supported.

Crystal's pimp was an optometrist named Paul, and she introduced him to both Robert and me. The two men became instant friends, and they soon knew all about one another. Perhaps they did not suspect how close Crystal and I had become; otherwise they would have been more secretive.

Paul shared with Crystal some things he had learned about Robert's activities. Those things were so disturbing that, although she knew I would be devastated, she felt that I deserved to know the truth about my pimp, who was living it up on money that I degraded myself to earn. Crystal revealed to me what Paul had told her. Robert was indulging in a promiscuous lifestyle, wantonly involved with many women. The hours he supposedly was devoting to his sons and to looking after business opportunities were actually spent in licentious pursuits. The worst revelation from Crystal was that on a regular basis, Robert was entertaining a young woman in our apartment while I was out on the streets at night. According to Paul, the young woman was a student from Ulm, from where we had recently moved. Robert had been involved with her there, and he brought her to Munich after we moved there.

I also learned from Crystal that Robert's deviant lifestyle was common knowledge among other prostitutes and their pimps. He was out of town when I received all this revelation, so I decided to greet his return with a surprise party. Robert got home to find that I had gathered together several pimps that knew about his activities. Their characters were actually no better than Robert's but because of Crystal's testimony, I knew they were telling the truth. These men readily agreed to take part in my plan to confront Robert, because they hoped I would leave him and become part of their "stable." I was one of the most attractive and popular girls on the street, and more than likely I brought in more earnings than any of the others. What pimp wouldn't want to own me as one of his girls?

When I confronted Robert in front of his fellow pimps, he vigorously denied all the allegations and accused them of lying. One man responded to this charge by slugging Robert and declaring that by his betrayal he forfeited the right to have control of me and that he was taking over. The others joined in and gave Robert a severe beating. I finally convinced the defenders of my honor that they had done enough and that they had taught Robert a lesson he would not soon forget. After they had left and I had bathed his wounds, Robert assumed a contrite position on his knees before me and begged me to forgive him. He looked so pitiful and seemed so repentant that I could not withhold my mercy. So instead of using the opportunity to flee from him and turn from a life of prostitution, I foolishly forgave him and continued to submit to his control. I gave clear notification to all the other pimps that I was giving him another chance and that I was not available to anyone else.

Robert immediately became more attentive to me and suggested that I needed to take some time off and that we go on a vacation. In truth, I realized that he was actually being selfish in his suggestion, because he needed to recuperate from the beating he had received. However, I did indeed need to get off the streets. My emotions were shattered because of Robert's infidelity, and my body was in a dreadful state because I had become both anorectic and bulimic. During our time away, we agreed that we should make a new start in another city, where no one knew us. We decided on Frankfurt, the financial center of Germany.

In the fall of 1974 Robert and I moved into an apartment on the eighth floor of a high-rise building, with my income covering the expenses as usual. I also secured another apartment for the purpose of entertaining my customers. Crystal and Paul moved to Frankfurt at the same time, and I continued to be close friends with them. Robert kept the apartment in Munich, where he lived when he was not in Frankfurt. Actually, as time later revealed, this was his back-up security. I should have known better than to entrust all the property to him, but up to this time I was completely under his control.

Frankfurt was, and still remains, one of the most expensive cities in the world, and I was soon making more money than I could have ever imagined. By this time I had developed a growing distrust of Robert, and I deceived him concerning my earnings. I held back a sizeable amount each day, stashing it away in various hiding places. For a while, Robert was none the wiser, because he attributed the decrease to the fact that I was just getting started in a new city, and it would take time to build up a large clientele. He didn't know that I was making far more in Frankfurt than in the other cities.

As an example of my new opportunities, a rich unmarried

businessman from Amsterdam always sought my services when he came to Frankfurt, and every time he generously rewarded me. On one occasion he asked me why a classy and beautiful woman like me was engaged in prostitution. I gave him the same story that I had been using for years, but no longer believed: "It's only temporary. I'm saving money to buy a boutique." He even paid me an enormous sum to spend a week with him in Amsterdam. There he took me to the most exclusive restaurants and clubs and social functions, introducing me to his friends and business associates as his girl friend. I didn't mind the deception at all, because I was getting paid for having a great vacation.

Robert's suspicions concerning my income soon began to grow. He made a weekly trip to Frankfurt from Munich just to collect my earnings, and he wondered why I wasn't getting more. I always explained that business was slow because of the bad weather and various other reasons. Crystal would give him the same story, and that put him off for a while.

Frankfurt was experiencing some foul weather that season, and there were many nights that I didn't work at all. On one such night I was enjoying a leisurely time in a coffee house, when a couple of swarthy men came to my table and introduced themselves. Naturally, I thought they were interested in soliciting my services, but they actually were just being friendly and wanted conversation. They presented themselves as Greeks who were in the fur business and invited me to visit their wholesale place, which I did. We soon became very special friends and enjoyed dinners, shows and other activities together. Although they quickly perceived that I was a prostitute, they never asked for sexual favors. I was certain that they were homosexual partners, but I still enjoyed their friendship, and with them I could forget what I was.

One of my friends was named Panagiotis, which means, "all-holy," although I don't think he lived up to it. One day Panagiotis took me to their place of business, saying that he had a birthday gift for me. The surprise was a black diamond mink coat, and when I put it on, Panagiotis swore that I looked like a million. He later added a big mink belt to the coat to make it even more stunning and expensive.

Although my Greek friends were legal, through them I learned that Frankfurt had a very active black market trade in the fur and leather business. They even directed me to one underworld business, where I bought a mink coat and several leather ones at a fraction of the retail value. I had just found a way to supplement my earnings.

I spent more and more time with my expanding circle of Greek friends, visiting bars and social events. There was always something going on in the Greek community, and for me it was an escape from the dread of practicing my profession. At the same time, however, I was becoming increasingly depressed, and I was turning to alcohol more than ever to find comfort. I was terribly lonely, and I hated what I was doing. But I didn't know how to get out, and even if I did, I was fearful because it was the only way I knew to make a lot of money for my future.

One night I stumbled back to my apartment, weary from having entertained clients for several hours and intoxicated from drinking myself into a stupor. I went into the bathroom and looked at myself in the mirror, shocked at the reflection. I found it hard to believe that I had come to such a point that I looked so bad. I shut my eyes at the sight, clenched my fists and cried out, "If there is a God in heaven, get me out of this lifestyle!" It really wasn't a prayer as such, but it came from the depths of my soul, and God must have received it as a genuine prayer.

Soon after this outcry, I was in a Greek bar, where I met a nice gentleman from Bulgaria who spoke fluent German. For some reason, I felt that if I unloaded my misery on him he would understand. So I spilled my guts and told him my whole sordid story, concluding with my desire to get out. He listened patiently with genuine interest and sympathy, and when I finished he began to encourage me. He assured me that there was a way out and that I could have a better life. He proceeded to tell me of a Bulgarian couple who were in the jewelry business and who were his close friends. They were planning to immigrate to the United States, where they felt certain that they would enjoy a better life. Maybe I could join them. Unknown to both of us, he was speaking a prophecy.

After several months in Frankfurt, I was ready to get away from Robert completely. The humiliating beating he received when he was exposed cautioned him to be more careful with me, and he didn't come around me as much as before. He began spending most of his time in Munich, coming to Frankfurt only to get money. His visits become so infrequent that I was soon working alone. By this time Robert was convinced that I had a boy friend, because there was such less money. He didn't protest, because he was fearful that he might get beat up again. I knew that he was nothing but a cheap louse that lived on my earnings, and I lost all respect for him, as well as the love I once felt.

I was certain that my name was on the deeds of each of the condominiums we had bought (with my money), but I soon discovered that Robert had sold most all of our real estate holdings, forging my signature to do so. I was determined to recover some of my money from the property investments, so I decided to confront him. My mother was in disagreement with me and advised me to forget the whole thing. I finally talked her into going with me, so on the way to Munich I picked her up.

When Robert opened the door of our apartment in response to my belligerent knocking, he registered surprise to see two angry and determined women standing there. Without any greeting or preamble of any kind, I announced the purpose of our visit: "I have come to get what rightfully belongs to me!"

There was just a brief hint of bewilderment on his face before he burst out in an evil laughter that chilled my blood. As he was slamming the door in our faces, he sneered, "You're too late! I've already sold it off!"

Now my chilled blood was suddenly boiling at the despicable announcement I had just heard. In a cowardly underhanded way, I had been robbed of a small fortune, not to mention the hundreds of thousands of Deutsch marks Robert had taken from me over the years. In my fury I started screaming curses and tried to kick the door down. Inquisitive neighbors were looking out their doors before Mother got my attention and calmed me down and finally persuaded me to leave. "It's worth everything you lost just to get rid of him," she said. "Now you can get your life back in order."

Over the next few days I brooded over the situation and finally decided to take legal action. I had sacrificed my dignity and physical and emotional health for this man and I had degraded myself to the lowest scale of womanhood because of him. I had nothing left, but I was determined to try to regain some of it. My first step was to go to the police and file formal charges against my pimp.

After I spilled out the whole sordid story of how Robert had forced me into prostitution and exercised total control over me, the authorities wasted no time in issuing a warrant for his arrest. I should not have been surprised to learn it, but I did not know at the time that Robert was a hot suspect on the police watch list because of a past history of involvement in illegal activities. They were most pleased that they now had enough evidence to bring him to trial.

The trial lasted only one day, and I was the chief witness against Robert. I had plenty of indisputable evidence, including names of people and places and written records. Some of my friends who had been victimized into prostitution corroborated my testimony, exposing Robert as a professional con artist who lived on the earnings of those under his control.

Robert could offer only a lame and weak defense, with no proof that he had been supporting himself with a steady job. When the prosecutor asked him how he spent his time and earned a living, he replied, "Well, I spend most of my time with my wife and children." His explanations were so transparently false and so ludicrous that even the judge almost laughed. Among other charges, he was found guilty of perjury, embezzlement and pimping and received a sentence of several years of imprisonment. As he was led from the courtroom in chains, he glared at me with a look of demonic hatred that promised revenge. That was the last time I saw him, and I have never regretted that day.

Soon after I was away from Robert, I gradually began phasing out of prostitution. I didn't know what I was going to do, and I had no prospects for a job. To occupy my time, I starting visiting more frequently the nightclub where I had met Mitch, the Bulgarian businessman I mentioned earlier. Ever since I had met him, he had been a source of encouragement to me, and now that all ties to Robert were broken, he convinced me that I should get out of prostitution completely and immediately, and he offered to help me. I had cried out to God for a change in my lifestyle, and perhaps this was part of the answer that I so desperately sought.

Mitch had told me about the Bulgarian couple who planned to immigrate to the United States. Now he announced that he was joining them in a partnership and that he would be going with them. By this time we had become very close, and he asked me to be a part of his future plans. Everything was in motion for their move to America, and they all had visas to enter the country in November of 1976, only a few weeks away. Mitch said that they could add me to their company as the secretary and that I should have no trouble getting a visa. I was thrilled at the prospect of beginning a new life far away from my shameful and miserable past, so I readily agreed. I was overwhelmed by his concern and generosity, but he confessed that he loved me and wanted to take care of me. He began to shower me with expensive gifts of jewelry and clothing. I felt that there really must be a God in heaven.

To say that my mother was delighted when I brought Mitch to my hometown of Wemding to introduce him to the family would be an understatement. She was absolutely captivated by him, recognizing him as a fine man, and she was filled with gratitude that he had proposed marriage to me and that I would be delivered from the life that I had been leading. Without any questions, she joyously gave her approval of our plan to relocate in the United States. In fact, she came to Frankfort to help me prepare for the transition, assisting me in selecting furniture and other items that we would ship to America.

Mitch and the Bulgarian couple had already secured their visas to immigrate to the United States, so they all accompanied me to the American embassy, where I would apply for my own visa as secretary of the company. However, to our extreme disappointment, I received a visa that was valid for only six months. We wanted to establish a new life in the United States, and I might as well not even go if I could stay for only half a year.

I submitted another application and then a third, but the results were the same. Our departure date was drawing near, and I was desperate. For some reason, I decided to apply once more, only this time I would go alone, and instead of going to the embassy, I would go to the American consulate in Wiesbaden. There I met a very kind lady who took my application, passport and supporting documentation and went into her office, leaving me to wait in suspense for the next hour in the reception area. Finally, she returned with a smile and handed over an envelope containing my passport and other documents and wished me a good trip to America.

I had already suffered three disappointments, so I didn't even bother to look at my documents before hurrying to a nearby restaurant to join Mitch and the others. "Well, how did it go?" they asked. I replied that I evidently had received a visa, since the lady had dismissed me with such a positive and favorable comment. They couldn't believe that I had not even looked at the visa. As they crowded around me, I slowly and fearfully opened my passport. When we saw the stamped visa, we could only gasp in surprise. I had been granted a four-year business visa! No one could possibly receive such an approval in only one hour, and someone remarked, "How lucky you are!" At that time I agreed that luck was on my side. Later on, after I had begun my spiritual journey, I realized that luck had nothing to do with my experience. The providence of God was shaping and controlling my destiny.

We shipped our belongings, including four cars, in a container on a freighter bound for California and soon afterward we boarded a jet for Los Angeles. I wish I could describe the flight as a quiet time of grateful reflection on all the good things that had been happening to me and on what surely would be a bright future. However, I can only remember that the long trip was more like a party, with lots of drinking and smoking.

After clearing immigration and customs in Los Angeles, we went to Long Beach, where we would await the arrival of our container by staying in a motel operated by a German family. My old life was behind me forever, and I would soon be married to a prosperous and wonderful man. Could the future be any better?

The ship carrying our container did not arrive for several weeks. We spent the time looking for an apartment and making business contacts. The Bulgarians knew some wealthy people in the jewelry business, and they always picked us up in their limousine to take us to meetings. Things were looking better all the time.

By the time the container arrived with our belongings, Mitch and I had located a large apartment in Los Angeles. For a while I kept busy unpacking, arranging the furniture and decorating the apartment, while Mitch was occupied with business developments. It wasn't long before I ran out of activities to pass away the time, and I began to suffer boredom. Mitch was gone most of the time during the week, and I was not included in the business dealings. I knew no one in the city, I didn't know my way around, and I had no way of getting there even if I did know the way. I felt sorely neglected, and I took out my frustration by complaining to Mitch about the treatment he was giving me. To make matters worse, I felt ignored and excluded when our Bulgarian friends visited, because they all spoke in their own language, not a word of which I could understand. To compensate for my loneliness, I began drinking, which only intensified the problems that were becoming more severe.

How many people start on the road to alcoholism by drinking alone in self-pity instead of trying to find something constructive to do?

My discontent grew into misery, and my arguments with Mitch became more frequent and more tempestuous. After one shouting match that was particularly volcanic, I challenged Mitch to either change the way things were or to leave. He chose to leave. One day I left the apartment to spend some time in a nearby tavern. I returned to find an apartment stripped of half its furnishings, with no Mitch and no note of explanation. I never saw him again.

I was on my own in a strange country, with few resources, friends and job skills. Although I had learned a little English while I was attending the business school in Germany, I realized that I had to become more proficient in the language if I were to secure a decent job. Therefore, I enrolled in an advanced English class at Hollywood High School. During that time I met a few friends, including a French-Canadian couple named John and Elise. On several occasions I attended a Catholic church with them, the first time I had been inside a church in years.

Soon I ventured forth into the job market. My first job was as a waitress in a trendy restaurant that specialized in barbequed ribs and chicken. In very little time I earned enough money to rent a one-room apartment in a nice area of Los Angeles. At this restaurant I had my first encounter with a cult. A group called the Church of Love rented one of the several banquet rooms in the establishment, and I regularly served them. They invited me to attend one of their meetings, and I accepted, not knowing that they were heavily involved in occultist practices such as fortune telling. As naïve as I was, I actually paid money to a woman who supposedly could tell my future. That first meeting was enough for me.

During my three-year employment at the barbeque restaurant, I heard a lot about a famous landmark in Hollywood, the Brown Derby.

This place was a favorite of the movie and television industry, and among the patrons at any given time were numerous celebrities. I discovered that that the Brown Derby was under German ownership, so I applied for a job there, mostly as a lark. To my surprise, they hired me, the only female among the host of men waiters. I worked in the lounge, serving meals and drinks from the bar. The customers loved me, mostly because of my strong German accent, and my regulars always asked for me. I soon became acquainted with a lot of Hollywood stars.

One would think that things were going great for me. I was making good money, I had a nice apartment, and I was wearing fine clothing. However, I was still lonely and I had never conquered my drinking problem. As a matter of fact, I was drinking more than ever, and it was having an effect on my work performance, even though I did most of my drinking after hours. Finally, my supervisor gave me notice, making it clear that it was because of my drinking habits. One of my loyal customers was the manager of a local television station that was the flagship station of a national network. This man graciously gave me an excellent recommendation, typed and personally signed on the letterhead of the network.

I took a few days off after leaving the Brown Derby and engaged in some heavy barhopping. At one bar I met Norma, a friendly woman dressed in a very distinct masculine fashion. I thought little of her choice of clothing, because it seemed that any style was acceptable in Hollywood. We began to hang out together, drinking and eating at various bars and restaurants and going to shows. At one bar that I frequented, the bartender, Jimmy, took me aside and warned me to drop my friendship with Norma, because she was a lesbian. I didn't believe him, because Norma had never made any inappropriate advances toward me, so I disregarded his warning.

Norma and I continued to have an enjoyable social relationship.

I learned that her mother was one of the most successful and highly sought after lawyers in the city. On one occasion I accepted Norma's invitation to visit her home, a huge exquisite mansion in a very exclusive neighborhood. While we were there, she introduced me to Tarot cards. I was somewhat uneasy, but intensely fascinated, when she spread out the cards and declared that they showed that I would have a very prosperous future.

One night Norma and I spent the evening drinking our way through one bar after another, after which we went to my apartment. There we continued our heavy drinking until I passed out. I didn't remember getting to bed, but I woke up to find Norma in bed with me, fondling me. Evidently, she had drugged one of my drinks. I was disgusted by her advances and pushed her away. She responded by talking about how good I looked and how I had encouraged this relationship by going out with her. My increasing anger seemed only to fuel her passion, and she began to force herself on me physically. With more strength than I realized I had, I overcame her and pushed her out of my apartment.

A few days later, I met my friend Elise, and she expressed concern over my health. She remarked that I was unusually pale and that I looked swollen, and she insisted that I see a doctor. Fortunately, my health insurance from my previous job was still effective, so I went to a doctor for a check-up. The report of my physical condition was not good. I had a bad liver, which caused the swelling, and I was suffering from bulimia and anorexia. I was too ashamed to talk to the doctor about my drinking problem, but I think he detected it and just didn't mention it out of kindness. He probably would have been kinder if he had given me a stern lecture about it.

The report concerning my physical condition did nothing to lessen my drinking habit. If anything, I was drinking more than ever. I started working in another bar/restaurant, and the environment didn't help at all. I realized that I had a severe problem, but I didn't know what to do about it. I was absolutely powerless and I couldn't stop drinking. I had only one resource, and I used it. I cried out to God, admitting my helplessness and asking for deliverance.

Soon thereafter I came home from work one day and found a card on the floor by my door. Printed on the card was Luke 1:37: "For with God nothing will be impossible." There was also a name and a phone number. I didn't know the Scripture, but because it mentioned God I felt a surge of hope and called the number. A lady's kind voice answered and I made an appointment with her for counseling. I was excited, feeling that I had found God.

When I arrived for my appointment, I discovered that the woman was a Hindu called Madam Omar and that she claimed to be a psychic. She was a soft-spoken middle-aged lady who seemed so sincere that I had no idea that I was being deceived. Around the room were statuettes of Mary, Jesus on the cross, Buddha, and various other religious artifacts. She apparently was trying to cover all the bases. We talked together and I told her all about my past and my current drinking problem. She was very sympathetic and promised to pray for me with a secret prayer ritual that was guaranteed to bring results. There was no mention of money, and I made a second appointment. We went through the same routine, and I made a third appointment. This time she told me that I would have to give her $800.00 to cover the first two sessions and that she would not see me again without payment. I was distraught, so I frantically saved enough money to go back to Madam Omar. When I asked her if she would teach me the prayer ritual that was supposed to help me, she replied that it was a secret ritual that only she could pray. She also told me that I should continue to save money for future appointments. By then it began to dawn on me that Madam Omar was a con artist and that I had been taken. I felt an evil presence in the house, and it wasn't just the mouse that I saw scurrying across the room. I felt unclean and a tremendous oppression weighed heavily upon me. I couldn't wait to get out of the place, and I never went back.

It goes without saying that my so-called counseling sessions with Madam Omar proved to be fruitless. In fact, I was worse off than before, and I couldn't stop my downward spiral. I kept trying to give up drinking, and every hour without liquor was a victory. One Friday evening I arrived home sober, proud of myself for bypassing my favorite bar. I could not remember a previous day when I had not had a drink.

I fixed a late supper, washed and dried the dishes and prepared for bed. As usual, I opened my bedroom window a few inches to let in some air and put earplugs in my ears to shut out the noise of traffic. It was well past midnight when I retired, and I fell asleep immediately. At some point I was jolted awake from a deep sleep by my mother's voice screaming, "Rosie! Rosie! Rosie!" In alarm I sat upright in the bed and saw a man standing at the foot of the bed. He had removed the screen from the window and crawled into the room. Because of the earplugs I heard not a sound. The intruder was wearing a stocking mask, and he was holding the wet towel that I had used to dry the dishes. He came toward me with the towel stretched end to end in both hands, as though he would use it to strangle me. My reaction wasn't quite what he expected, and it completely startled him. Instead of being scared speechless or whimpering in defenseless submission, I threw the bed covers back, jumped onto the floor and ran toward him, screaming with all the volume my lungs would allow. He fell backwards, then turned and fled out the same way he had entered.

He surely wasn't afraid of me, but he must have considered that my screams alerted the entire apartment complex. I notified the manager, who then called the police. A quick inventory revealed that the burglar had taken my television set, my purse, and several items of jewelry. As he was fleeing he took the car keys out of my purse and got away in my car. For the next eight days I rode the bus to work. Then my car was found in downtown Los Angeles, and after their investigation the police return it to me.

In retrospect, I felt that this incident was an act of revenge on the part of Madam Omar after I dropped out of her bogus counseling program. She had been calling me at the bar where I worked, harassing me and warning me that dangerous things awaited me if I did not continue coming to her.

I was actually frightened by what this woman was capable of doing, and I contemplated going back to see her. However, about that time I met Becky, a clerk in a clothing store. I walked into the shop and heard beautiful music playing. I was unfamiliar with it, but by the lyrics I knew that it was Christian music. I asked the clerk, Becky, about it and she confirmed that it was Christian music and that she was a Christian. But I had never heard anybody who claimed to be a Christian talk like she did. It was obvious that she didn't just know about God; she actually seemed to have a personal intimate relationship with Him. I felt drawn to her, and I knew I could trust her. I needed to confide in someone about Madam Omar and to get some advice about what to do, so I told Becky about my visits to the psychic. She told me that Madam Omar was a deceitful witch who served Satan and whose purpose was to extort money from desperate people like me. She also told me that God would protect me and that I had nothing to fear. She was very convincing, and I believed her.

Becky was so kind and genuine that I wanted to learn more about her and her Christian experiences. We began a friendship and saw each other quite often. Through her I learned that Jesus Christ is a living reality and that we can know Him personally. At first I couldn't comprehend all that she was saying to me, so she patiently began at my level of understanding and shared whatever I could receive. She told me about God's power and that miracles still happen. In fact, she had experienced a miraculous healing. She had been blind in her right eye, and the Lord restored her sight after an evangelist prayed for her. She told me that I could learn a lot by watching Christian television, particularly Trinity Broadcasting Network (TBN). I had never heard of such a network, but, enthused by Becky's testimony, I called the cable company and added TBN to my programming. Some dramatic changes were about to take place in my life.

Before my conversation with Becky about Madam Omar, I had actually saved $500, with the intention of going back to see the witch. Now that I clearly saw the truth about evil deception, I decided to send the $500 to TBN. Becky had just begun talking to me about what it meant to be a Christian, and I was listening with an open heart and mind. I had not yet experienced salvation in the "born again" way that Becky described, but I was eagerly searching for God and I wanted to give something to His work. Some of the speakers at TBN talked about "planting seeds" and God's blessings, so I sent the $500.

What happened next wasn't exactly what I expected. I was on my way home from work late one night and missed the exit sign from the freeway. I had just passed my exit when I realized my mistake, so I pulled over to the right side and stopped. I had come only a short distance past the exit, so I thought I could slowly back up to the exit. I did indeed make it back to the exit, but before I could change gears to leave the freeway, another driver, traveling at a high rate of speed, wanted to use the same exit. He crashed into my car, totaling both vehicles. Fortunately, I was only bruised and shaken and the other driver suffered only minor injuries. The accident was my fault, and I didn't have enough insurance to cover all the damages. I had to hire an attorney to represent me, and it cost me a lot of money to settle the matter.

But I had just planted a seed of $500 to the Lord's work! What was happening? You can only imagine the doubts that came over me, but I knew that I had only myself to blame for a senseless accident. I could not blame God for what happened. In fact, I couldn't even blame the devil. Later, after I became a Christian, I realized that the seed that I had planted into the ministry of TBN became a covenant protection over my life, and God had spared my life again.

Becky was patient and faithful in sharing with me about the love of God and the way of salvation, and she encouraged me to continue watching Christian programs. One night I was watching *The 700 Club*, hosted by Pat Robertson. The testimonies and the teaching that I heard got through to me, so I was ready when Pat instructed viewers who wanted to be saved to pray with him. I prayed the sinner's prayer with him and asked Jesus to save me and to come into my heart. At that moment I was born again and became a new creature in Christ! I could not explain it, but I knew I was cleansed of all the past and that I was a new person.

Pat suggested that those who prayed with him to be saved should call Christian Broadcasting Network (CBN), the producers of *The 700 Club*. He said that if we didn't get an answer right away, we should keep trying. I called and called and called—for hours. It didn't occur to me that there was a time difference of three hours between Virginia, where CBN is located, and California, and that it was the wee hours of the morning on the East coast. Finally, a kind lady answered and prayed with me and gave me much encouragement and instructions about what to do next. My happiness was beyond description.

When Christ came into my life and I experienced a new birth, everything became different. I did not know then that "If anyone is in Christ, he is a new creation; old things have passed away; behold all things have become new" (2 Cor. 5:17). I only knew that I saw everything in a new light. I saw the trees differently; the flowers seemed to be more beautiful; the singing of the birds was more melodic. All of creation opened up to me, and I had a new understanding of life. My lifestyle changed; my relationships changed. I had a new hope of life. What I had been searching for was becoming real. It was Jesus, and I realized the meaning of what Jesus said in John 14:6: "I am the way, the truth, and the life. No one comes to the Father except through Me." My previous life of utter degradation as a prostitute was over. I later found the Scripture that told me that despite what I had been in the past, I was now a pure virgin before Christ (2 Cor. 11:2). I wept joyful tears as I marveled at God's redeeming grace. How radical was the change in my life? For years I had prostituted myself, but now God looked upon me as a chaste virgin. I had a new start, a new life. I was truly born anew, and the blood of Jesus wiped away all the sordid things of my past. I had a completely new life ahead of me, and I would live it in Christ.

Not long after my conversion I attended an outdoor crusade led by Arthur Blessitt, the worldwide cross-carrying evangelist. This was a very special event for me, joining thousands of other believers and having the opportunity to meet a great servant of God in person. Arthur's boldness and the dynamic message of the cross that he presented had a profound impact upon me, and I responded to the altar call in order to make my profession of faith public before the huge crowd of witnesses. Arthur laid hands on me and prayed over me. While he was praying I felt a special anointing coming upon me.

Although I had received Jesus into my life and my spirit was healthy, my physical body was still stricken with various ailments. Most of the time I dealt with severe pain in my stomach and other internal organs. I knew that my liver had been damaged by my drinking habits, and I had no desire to go back to that lifestyle. God had delivered me from alcoholism so I was no longer drinking, even though I still served liquor in my work. My new lifestyle brought mockery and persecution from some of the other waiters in the bar/lounge where I worked, but a few of them respected me for the stand I was taking. I became a strong witness for the Lord, both to co-workers and customers, openly sharing with them how Christ had changed my life. I suppose I was sometimes too direct and vocal, because some of regular customers began to avoid me. Even so, I knew I was planting seeds in their lives. I even witnessed to my boss, who was an alcoholic. He saw the difference in my life, and he was especially attracted to my new happiness.

During a break in one of my evening shifts in the summer of 1984, I made a quick trip to the post office for stamps. The Olympic games were being held in Los Angeles, and signs had been posted all over the city, giving directions to the different venues. However, the signs also created a lot of confusion. While I was driving back to work from the post office, a cab driver crashed into my car. The accident was clearly his fault, but he blamed me and later brought forth false witnesses to support his version of what happened. The police came to investigate the accident and wrote a report, and then they took me to the place of my employment. I ignored my supervisor's inquiry concerning my obvious severe distress as I rushed into the dressing room to change into my uniform. Suddenly I heard the word of God coming up in my spirit: "Call upon Me in the day of trouble: I will deliver you, and you shall glorify Me" (Psalm 50:15). This was the first time in my life that God's word came alive in me, and it brought me total peace from my fear and distress. I was a different person as I walked out of the dressing room into the lounge. My supervisor saw the difference and knew that I had experienced something real and dramatic.

The cab driver that collided with my car brought suit against me, and a date for the hearing was set. Shortly before that date, I attended a meeting at which the minister was Dick Mills, who was noted for his effective use of Scripture in prophetic pronouncements. At one point during the meeting he pointed to the side of the auditorium where I was seated and announced, "Anyone on this side who is involved in a court case will have the case dismissed." That prophecy came to pass. In spite of the cab driver's lies and the false testimonies of his witnesses, the decision of the court went against him and he had to pay all the expenses. Case dismissed! Two weeks after the court hearing, I bought a car that was far better than the one that had been wrecked. I got it at a ridiculously low price from a Christian missionary who was returning to the field.

As a new Christian, I knew that I needed the fellowship and instruction of a strong church that believed and preached the Bible in order that I might grow in the faith. I found such a church in the historic Angelus Temple, which had been founded by Aimee McPherson. I joined the church and was baptized by immersion in water.

The church had planned a celebration late on July 4, complete with fireworks, barbeque, and entertainment. While I was getting ready to leave, I had my television on the TBN channel. Oral Roberts was the guest on whatever program was showing at the time. He gave a biblical teaching on the baptism in the Holy Spirit and declared that all believers in Christ could have that experience. Then he instructed all viewers who wanted to receive the baptism in the Holy Spirit to release their faith to receive while he prayed. While Oral was praying the Spirit of God came upon me, and I began to speak in an unknown tongue. I began to cry tears of joy, and then the tears turned to laughter and praise. I couldn't stop speaking and singing in tongues and praising God, alternatively crying and laughing.

I was so caught up in the Spirit that I completely forget about the church outing, until it suddenly hit me that I was already an hour late. It really didn't matter to me, because I was enraptured by the joy and presence of the Holy Spirit. When I finally arrived, some of my new friends came running to me expressing concern, because they had repeatedly called me without an answer. Then they looked at me and exclaimed, "You're shining! What has happened to you?" I gladly shared my experience.

Not long after I joined Angelus Temple, I met Alice, a prophetess in the church who was a graduate of both Oral Roberts University and Kenneth Hagin's Rhema Bible College. She became a wonderful friend, counselor and instructor to me. I began to attend faithfully her weekly Saturday morning prayer meetings, where I learned much from her teachings about praying and confessing the word of God in our lives. Some time after we met, Alice told me that God had pointed me out to her and told her that she was to bring me under her wings and mentor me as I grew into mature discipleship.

I had a great deal to learn, because I knew nothing about the Bible and the Christian life beyond my catechism classes. In one church service I picked up one of the little envelopes from the rack on back of the pew in front of me. The printing on the envelope indicated that it was for tithes and offerings. I had no idea what a tithe was, so I asked Alice. She explained to me the biblical teachings about giving a tenth of your income to the Lord and how He would multiply your gifts and bring many blessings. I began to tithe, and the word of God proved to be true as I experienced constant blessings, financial and otherwise.

I was still dealing with some issues from my old life, such as smoking heavily. Alice was strict but patient with me as she loved and encouraged me in my growth. She and the prayer group ministered personally to me throughout this period of my early Christian life, leading me to renounce all the things that had been part of my old life, such as involvement in witchcraft, the horoscope, sexual sins, alcoholism, tobacco, depression, etc. The list of evils in my life was very long, but through the ministry of my friends, the Lord totally delivered me of all of them.

In the church services and prayer meetings I saw miraculous displays of God's power, and the teachings of the pastors and outstanding guest preachers made the Bible come alive to me. The word of God became part of my daily existence, and I could not devour enough of it.

*But you shall receive power when the Holy Spirit has come upon you, and you shall be witnesses to Me in Jerusalem, and in all Judea and Samaria, and to the end of the earth* (Acts 1:8).

I diligently attended all the Saturday morning prayer meetings led by Alice, as well as other services in the church. I was growing stronger in faith and knowledge every day, but I was still somewhat hesitant when Alice called to tell me that she could not be at the next prayer meeting and asked me to lead the meeting. I was humbled by her request and I appreciated her confidence in me, but I responded that I was a baby Christian and I hardly knew how to pray. How could I lead a group of people so much more mature in the faith than I?

With Alice's assurance that the Holy Spirit would help and direct me, I consented to lead the meeting. However, I almost faltered when I saw the gathering of about 25 people, representing more than a dozen nationalities and ethnic groups. Then I realized that we were all one in Christ, united by the indwelling of the Holy Spirit in each of us and by the common purpose of glorifying and serving the Lord.

We began by singing choruses of praise to God, and then we prayed. The prayers intensified as we prayed in unison, some in tongues, some in English, and others in various native languages. But God heard and understood each of us. We prayed for individual needs, for the world, for the country and its officials, for the city, for the church and its staff, and for many other needs. Best of all, however, was the praise we offered up to the Lord for His righteousness and grace and for His bountiful gifts. The presence of God was so strong that I believe that if I had opened my eyes I would have seen Him standing in our midst. I know that angels were present, joining us in worship. Through praying in the Spirit, the Lord showed me what to do, and the power of God fell upon us. People testified, prophesied and quoted Scripture as the Spirit prompted them. But when a lady began quoting Psalm 34, we could no longer contain ourselves. The room erupted with songs and shouts of praise as we exalted the Lord. Conviction came on some people who confessed and were delivered from various habits and attitudes. Some were healed of physical ailments and emotional problems. I left that glorious meeting with far more courage and faith than when I entered.

At Easter in 1985, a Catholic lady with whom I worked invited me to go with her to a sunrise service at the Hollywood Bowl. I had never been to anything like that, so I eagerly accepted the opportunity. I was so excited that I could not sleep after getting home from work on Saturday night. We left at 4:00 a.m., which in the old days of my life was about the time I would be getting home. We arrived early enough to get great seats close to the stage. Paul Crouch, president of TBN, emceed the event, which was televised by the network. The next Sunday at church many people came to me and told me they had seen me on television.

I was still working in the bar/lounge area of the restaurant. I had such a happy demeanor that some of the regulars who knew me would often say, "Rose, you must be in love." I always took such comments as an opportunity to witness for Christ, so I would respond, "I am in love—

with Jesus Christ. Let me tell you about Him." They didn't always listen, but they all knew that there had been a radical change in my life. Every day presented new opportunities to witness, and I took advantage of all of them. I know that good seeds were planted in many hearts ready to receive, but the results are known only in heaven.

One evening I was serving a lovely couple and their young daughter. She was a beautiful young lady, but her eyes were crossed. Compassion welled up within me, and with supernatural boldness I shared with them about the love of God and His healing power. Prompted by the Holy Spirit, I asked the parents if I could take their daughter to a private area and pray for her. They readily consented, and I led the girl to the ladies powder room. There we closed our eyes and I held her hands and prayed a simple but intense prayer for healing, calling upon the mercy of God and claiming the authority of the name of Jesus and the word of God. After the brief prayer we looked into each other's eyes. Her eyes were completely normal, healed by the power of God.

Not everyone was pleased by what happened. While I was praying, another waitress saw what was going on and reported to the manager that I was praying for people. My defense was that I only prayed with the consent of the people involved and that it was always in private. Regardless, I became the butt of jokes and endured mockery and cruel comments. The grace and peace of God kept me from anger and retaliation. One night I had a vision in which I saw many people standing in a big circle, and I called out, "How many people need to be saved?" Not one person responded, and they all remained lifeless. Once more I cried out the same question, with the same lack of response. That vision had a great impact on me, showing me God's desire that all should be saved. I thought of the shepherd who left the 99 and went after the one lost sheep. God doesn't want even one individual to perish.

One Sunday evening a group of about 20 people from a Catholic church, including two priests, came to the restaurant for dinner. Most of the group drank beer, but one of the priests had one highball after another during the course of the meal. It saddened me to see him indulging in so much hard liquor, and having been in the same situation, I felt compassion for him. As the meal was ending, I had the opportunity to share with the priest about my deliverance from alcoholism and I witnessed to him and the others in the group about the new birth. I related the story of Nicodemus coming to Jesus in secret and how Jesus explained that you must be born again in order to enter the kingdom of God (John 3:3).

Many groups of young people came to the restaurant and they usually ordered several drinks with their meal, attempting to show how "cool" they were. I always told them about my history of alcoholism and how the Lord brought me out. Then I entreated them not to drink any more during the evening. Many heeded what I had to say and thanked me for sharing my testimony. When they returned to the restaurant they would ask for me.

One night I felt an overpowering urgency to witness to a waitress named Elsie and ask her to give her life to Christ. I had witnessed to her many times previously, but never with this compelling sense of imperativeness. The reason became apparent only two days later. A young lady driving under the influence of drugs ran a red light and broadsided Elsie's car, demolishing it and crushing her body. She was rushed to the hospital, where a medical time fought to save her life. When I heard the news I immediately called my church to pray for Elsie's salvation and healing. She survived, but she was in critical condition and remained in the hospital several months. When she was able to receive visitors, I went to see her. She expressed her gratitude to me for witnessing to her and related how in her darkest hour she remembered what I had told her about being saved. She called on the Lord to save her, and Christ came into her heart. When she left the hospital she was healed both physically and spiritually.

All this time I felt an increasing conviction that I should leave my job. Finally, I came to the full realization that God was leading me elsewhere and that I should step out on faith. I posted a notice on the bulletin board at my church that I was looking for a job, but it was several weeks before I had a response of any kind. A lady called to suggest that I might investigate the possibility of working for a certain school marketing company in Los Angeles. The company enlisted people to enroll in a government-funded program that would teach them skills in technical areas such as computer repair, telecommunications and the like.

The manager and other personnel at the restaurant were stunned when I gave my notice. I had been a popular fixture there for several years, and despite the fact that I was regarded as something of a fanatic, I was generally well liked. In fact, for many weeks afterward they were still calling to check on how I was doing and to ask if I wanted to come back.

I have to admit that at first it was quite tempting for me to return to work with which I was familiar and at which I earned good money. The reason was simple. I did not know that my new job paid no set salary; it was all by commission. I really had to learn to exercise strong faith every day, and it was a tough trial. In addition to the fact that I had no salary, I had to meet people and try to convince them to try to qualify for the training program. I received payment only when they passed a test and actually enrolled. I felt thoroughly intimidated. I had no problem talking to strangers about the Lord, but it's something else talking to them about an educational program. The enemy constantly harassed me by bringing up my past history and by trying to convince me that I was not competent to present the program in a persuasive manner. My confidence and self-esteem took a nosedive, especially when I received my first paycheck. After many hours of hard work each day for many days, I received $45.00. To make matters worse, many of the team members with whom I worked were very profane and corrupt. Most of them smoked marijuana, declaring it to be God's best weed because it was natural.

I was in a stern battle on earth, but I had heavenly resources. I memorized every Scripture verse I could find about fear; I prayed before leaving home that the Lord would prepare the way for me and that He would fill me with courage and enable me to present the program in an irresistible manner. I also repeated that prayer before each interview. I learned to confess the word of God and to rely on His faithfulness to His promises.

In retrospect, I can see that God had enrolled me in the classroom of faith, with the Bible as my textbook and the Holy Spirit as my teacher. I experienced many periods of discouragement, even to the point of despair, but I continually stood on the word of God and became a more devoted and disciplined student of the word. I was in a faith walk, depending on the daily provision of the Lord. I didn't always feel the reality of the biblical promises that I was confessing each day, but I would still speak them. And God faithfully fulfilled every promise.

One particularly grim day I saw a tiny sparrow skittering through the grass, pecking around for food. As I watched, Matthew 6:26 came to my mind: "Look at the birds of the air, for they neither sow nor reap nor gather into barns; yet your heavenly Father feeds them. Are you not of more value than they?" I started standing on this verse, knowing that God would provide for me even more than He did for birds. Many days I would spend hours in an unemployment office, talking to jobless people, showing them the program that I represented and trying to persuade them to check it out. God allowed this time of discipline in my life to help me learn and exercise faith.

Even though my paycheck was only $45.00 and Satan argued that I needed every cent of it, I gave beyond the tithe and contributed $5.00 to the church. I believed that God was my security, and I confessed the promise of Philippians 4:19 that He would supply my every need "according to the riches of His glory in Christ Jesus." The following week I saw a slight increase, and little by little over the succeeding weeks, things progressed and my earnings became larger. One week I made $800.

By that time my team had been transferred to Anaheim from Los Angeles, and I had up to an hour commute every day. As usual, I was witnessing to fellow workers, especially to John, my supervisor in Anaheim. Many times when I shared with him my testimony of salvation and deliverance from alcoholism and other kinds of bondage, he would just shake his head and ask, "Rose, what is going on with you?"

One Friday I arrived in Anaheim to find John in the lobby of our office building, waiting for me. When I walked in, he greeted me with the question, "Rose, will you pray for me?" I replied that of course I would, and I asked him what was the problem. He had spurs on both feet that were causing such excruciating pain that he could hardly walk, and his doctor did nothing but prescribe some ointment.

We went into John's office to pray. Before praying for his feet, I asked him if he would like to give his life to the Lord. He replied, "Yes, it's time, and I want to know God as you do." I led him in the sinner's prayer and then I started praying for his feet. The Holy Spirit granted me the gift of faith and caused the word of God to rise up within me. I boldly confessed the promises of God pertaining to healing, and proclaimed the declaration of 1 Kings 18:36 that He is God and that I was His servant doing these things at His word.

There was no immediate physical response, but the joyful and grateful expression on John's face gave evidence that God had truly touched him. With tears in his eyes, he thanked me. When we returned to work on Monday, John came running to me, shouting that God had totally healed his feet and that he had no more pain. Furthermore, he confessed that he had been a closet alcoholic, but God had completely delivered him and took from him all desire for drinking. But the most rewarding report of all was his testimony of a new birth.

The influencing factor that caused my supervisor, John, to become a Christian was the daily witness that I gave, by both word and example. At every opportunity I shared with my co-workers and others how God had changed my life and the lives of many others. They knew that they could come to me with their problems and that I would pray for and with them.

One of my German friends, a lady named Telse, is an example of how God was blessing others through my instrumentality. In the time that I had known her, I had not noticed any particular disability about her. One day, however, she revealed to me that she had been born with impairment in her left shoulder that restricted her from lifting her arm higher than her waist. I could only envision how such an infirmity made it difficult to perform her responsibilities at work and elsewhere. Telse responded that, like everyone else with a physical problem, she had learned to cope with it. I felt both compassion and faith rising within me, and I asserted that God was going to heal her. With that proclamation, I proceeded to lay hands on her and pray for the release of her arm. After we prayed I went into the kitchen to fix us some tea. I came back into the room to see Telse kneeling on the floor, with both arms lifted high in the air as she was praising God for her healing. For the first time in her life she could raise her left arm straight up, and she could not help screaming repeatedly, "Rosie, I'm healed; Rosie, I'm healed!"

In 1986 I became a regular supporter, or partner, of the Oral Roberts Ministry. I sent offerings every month and faithfully watched the daily telecast with Oral and Richard Roberts. Periodically, there were spiritual life seminars at Oral Roberts University, to which partners would be invited to attend. I received an invitation to one of the three-day seminars, with housing and meals provided free of charge. The only expense to me was my transportation to Tulsa and back, but God also arranged for my flight as well. My friend Telse had also received an invitation, and she paid for both our flights with money that her father had sent her as a gift. God has many ways to meet our needs!

After we arrived on the futuristic campus of ORU and checked into our room at one of the dormitories, we met many other people from all over the country who were attending the seminar. As we were walking through the lobby of the dorm on the way to dinner, we met two ladies who were having problems breathing, because Tulsa's high humidity was affecting their sinuses. They were suffering so much that they had decided not to attend the meeting at all. Emboldened by the Holy Spirit, I asked if I could pray for them, and they gladly agreed. As usual, I laid hands on them and spoke the word of God over them. The healing power of God came over them and they were instantly healed. That night they gave public testimonies of what happened to them.

At one of the meetings of the seminar, we were seated next to a lovely middle-aged couple. During the conversation that we enjoyed while we were waiting for the session to begin, the husband revealed that he had a severe hearing problem. I just had time to say, "You will receive your healing tonight," before the meeting started. After Richard Roberts taught from the Bible, he began a time of ministry. At one point he had a word of knowledge that someone's hearing was being restored. As he was announcing the healing, my new friend's ears popped, and he could hear clearly. He had just experienced a miracle, and he gladly stood and gave public testimony to it.

I didn't know it at the time, but my partnership with the Oral Roberts Ministries was to play a significant role during a trying time in my life. It began in 1985, when my sister Gerlinda called me with the news that our father was in serious condition at the hospital. Tests revealed that he had liver cancer, so advanced that there was no hope of recovery. I was devastated, and I desperately wanted to see him. However, for reasons I'll explain later, it was not prudent for me to leave the country at that time.

However, my brother Freddie, who was then living in San Francisco, had already planned to go to Germany for a class reunion, so he was able to visit our father. The report that he called back to me was shattering. According to the medical authorities, my father had only short months to live, and more likely only weeks. I was so numbed that all I could say in response was that I would pray. I hung up the phone and fell to my knees, groaning in the Spirit. A profound and urgent passion of intercession welled up inside of me, and I began battling for my father's life. Gradually, a heavenly peace descended upon me as Romans 8:28 resounded in my soul: "And we know that all things work together for good to those who love God, to those who are the called according to His purpose." In the quietness that followed, the Holy Spirit spoke to me most clearly: "No matter what you hear; no matter what they tell you; no matter what the situation looks like; stand on my word and praise Me."

This message aroused the spiritual warrior within me and I boldly and defiantly declared, "Satan, you cannot have my father, and he will not die!" Then I started thanking God for sparing my father's life, confessing aloud the promises of His word. I also reminded God that He had healed my liver, and I had drunk a lot more than my father had. That season of intercession concluded with a firm conviction in my soul that God had heard me and that all was well.

Over the next three or four weeks I continued steadfastly in prayer for my father, especially when driving to and from work and during pauses in the workday. I constantly prayed God's promises back to Him and made certain that my father's name, Franz Hackenberg, reached the throne room of heaven repeatedly. I declared to God that my father could not die, because he was not saved.

My faith grew stronger and I wrote a letter to Dad, filled with positive expressions of that faith. I pronounced that he would be going home and that he would be able to take care of his garden, ride his bicycle, tend to his pet rabbits, and take the walks that he enjoyed so much. I testified to him about how God had healed me from cancer and delivered me from acute alcoholism. Most importantly of all, I wrote to him about the plan of salvation and pleaded with him to surrender his life to the Lord.

I was actually speaking prophecy into my dad's life. He was soon dismissed from the hospital and resumed his normal lifestyle, especially tending his garden and indulging his usual hobbies.

It was 1987, and I was standing in faith on behalf of my father. Oral Roberts talked a lot about "Seed Faith," that is, when you have a need, you should sow a seed of faith and believe that God would meet the need. At that particular time, Oral and Richard were planning a trip to Israel, and they were taking with them prayer requests to pray over at an anointed service in the Holy Land. I sowed a seed of $77.00 into their ministry, believing God for my father's healing and salvation. Dad had already experienced a miracle, because he was still living two years after the doctors said he had only weeks to live. I was able to use this testimony to lead many people to the Lord. When my father did die at the age of

77, at God's appointed time instead of the time decreed by man, the cause was not cancer. It was a problem with his stomach. Some time after his death I had a dream in which I received a letter from him. In the letter Dad assured me that he was well, and he signed it, "With Love." To me, this dream was confirmation that my father was in heaven with the Lord.

78

The four-year business visa that I miraculously received when I came to the USA had now been expired for seven years, and I knew that I had to take steps to become a legal resident of the country. My friend Alice put me in contact with a Christian attorney who was very sympathetic and helpful to me. However, the process of becoming a legal resident was quite expensive, so I had to delay things until I could save enough money.

One day not long after the death of my father, Alice called me in a state of excitement. She had just heard the news on television that President Reagan had initiated a program of amnesty to illegal immigrants who had been in the country for ten years or more and who met certain requirements, such as having been gainfully employed. I met all the requirements, and to prove it I had a social security number, tax records and other documentation.

Alice felt very strongly that I should file an application for amnesty, so she accompanied me to the office of a Catholic charity that was handling applications. One obstacle that I faced was my desperate need to make a trip back to Germany to see my mother and take care of some things related to my father's death. Technically, I was without a country, and I had no passport. And I could not obtain a passport because I was not a citizen. If I left the United States as an illegal alien, it was highly unlikely that I could re-enter the country. Alice explained to the person in charge about my situation, but he told us that there was nothing they could do to help us and dismissed us.

I was devastated by this turn of events, and I was crying as we left the office. Just as we were exiting the building, a middle-aged lady, dressed in sophisticated business attire, was entering. Seeing my emotional state, she asked us what had happened in the office to upset me so much. "It's a long story," answered Alice.

"I've got time to listen," the woman kindly responded, "and perhaps I'll be able to help you." She then invited us to sit on a bench in the lovely garden on the grounds of the charity while we told our plight. Alice related all the details of my dilemma, concluding with the dreamful statement, "I wish they could have done something for my friend, Rose."

Our benefactor had listened patiently, and only after she heard our story did she identify herself as the head of the Catholic charity. She then gave us her business card and instructed us to call the number printed on it and make an appointment. She assured us that she would see to it that I would be granted amnesty, receive a passport and be allowed to travel to Germany.

Meeting this dear lady was not a coincidence; it was a supernaturally arranged miracle. She was true to her word, and all my documentation was rapidly completed. On June 24 I received my passport! Usually such a process was a long drawn out affair, and nobody was the recipient of special favors. However, the Lord promises "favor and high esteem in the sight of God and man" (Proverbs 3:4), and so my application was granted expeditiously.

There was an added feature to the process of receiving my new status. The charity director had put a woman named Ann in charge of handling my case, and I had several interviews with her over the next week. Ann had been in this particular office for only two months, having been transferred there from Washington, D.C. We discovered that she and Alice's sister Marilyn had once been very close friends, but they had lost contact with each other. Now, Alice and I were able to reconnect them.

I did not have the money to buy an airline ticket to Germany, but my brother Freddie came to my rescue and loaned me the money. I had not returned to my native country since I arrived in the USA eleven years before. When I left there, I was leaving behind a lot of shame and wreckage, but I had learned that even a change of countries could not wipe out the guilt that you carried inside, and it certainly could not make a new person of you. Only a new birth by the grace of God can cleanse a person from the stains of a life of wicked rebellion and bring complete deliverance. I had left Germany as a prisoner bound fast in the chains of sin, miserable and self-centered and wasting away. Now I was returning as a child of God, set free from all bondage and seeking to live a life pleasing to the Lord.

Before I boarded the plane, I prayed that the Lord would connect me with the right people and that I would have an opportunity to be a witness for Him. It's a very long flight from Los Angeles to Frankfort, and I didn't want to waste any time.

On the plane I found that my seatmate was a retired military officer, and we immediately struck up a conversation. He was easy to talk to, and before we left the coast of America, I was giving him my testimony of a changed life and describing to him to power and goodness of God. In turn, he opened up to me with his story of a life of uncertainty and frustration. Thirty thousand feet or so over the continent of Europe, my new friend looked at me and asked if I would pray with him that he might have the same experience that I had. I shared the simple plan of salvation with him, and he asked Jesus to save him. He walked off the plane as a different man than when he boarded.

My only regret in coming to Germany was that I had not arrived in time for my father's memorial service. However, I would be able to visit my family and friends, and I prayed that the Lord would use the trip to His glory. My sister Traudl met me at the airport. I had left Germany from this same airport years before, and things were totally different now, because I was seeing everything from a new perspective. Tears flooded my eyes as memories, both good and bad, rushed upon me. During the three-hour drive to Wemding along the familiar roads, Traudl brought me up to date on relatives, former classmates and other friends. I had ample opportunity to visit most of them during my three-week stay in Germany.

The reunion with my mother was joyous, but not without testing moments. In letters and telephone conversations, I had given reports to her of my new life in Christ, but she really had not comprehended what I was talking about. She was a devout Catholic, and she faithfully recited the rosary, attended mass, went to confession and observed all the church rites. Her experience of Christianity was an external, formal adherence to creeds and ceremonies, but she knew nothing of an intimate, living, personal moment-by-moment relationship with the Lord. Actually, she seemed to have a greater devotion to the priest than to Christ. She made regular confession to him and did whatever penance he prescribed. She made special dishes for him and kept him well supplied with liquor.

Now I show up carrying two Bibles that I spend a lot of time reading; sharing the wonderful things of God is just as normal in my conversation as discussing the weather; I'm witnessing to my relatives and friends and praying with them, and I am leading many of them into a confession of faith in Jesus as their personal Lord and Savior. My mother had a better understanding of me in my old life as a prostitute than in my current life as a committed Christian. Dedication to gods of greed, alcohol and lust she could fathom, but since she had never met anyone who displayed the devotion to Jesus Christ that I did, my conduct was beyond her comprehension. Consequently, she was suspicious of me, particularly when I would slip away to find privacy to pray with someone. She had come to the conclusion that I was a religious fanatic, and what was worse, part of a dangerous cult. She had more concern for me as an evangelical Christian than as a streetwalker. It would take a lot of time and prayer before she finally understood.

My visit to Germany was fruitful, and I had accomplished a great deal, besides enjoying being among people dear to me and in places familiar to me. I had taken care of some personal matters and I had led several friends and relatives to the Lord. Everyone marveled at the change in my life, even though a few entertained the same view as my mother and identified me with the Watchtower cult.

But now it was time to go home. Germany was no longer my country, and Wemding, where I had grown up, was no longer my home. I was not only an adopted child of God; I was an adopted child of the United States of America.

I faced some serious decisions upon my return. There was restlessness in my spirit concerning my employment, and I felt a release and knew peace only when I decided to leave the marketing company. They had been kind to me, and the head office had sent me a lovely plant when my father died. Now they sent me on my way with a very positive recommendation.

Not long after I resigned my former position, I began working for a private catering company operated by the Glendale Federal Bank of California. It was a first-class concern, and the workers were required to wear elegant, formal clothes at its events. I hosted three different departments, a small private room, a big dining room and the Gold Room for top executives. We entertained important politicians, bankers, doctors, attorneys and executives in all industries. There was very little stress related to this job, and I loved it, especially since the small number of employees provided the opportunity to build enjoyable relationships.

One of my coworkers was a homosexual named Jimmy. He knew my stance and he respected me, especially since I did not maintain a condemning attitude toward him or his lifestyle. He was actually a lot of fun, and I enjoyed his company. Sometimes we did outside catering at the beach in Palos Verdes. On such occasions, Jimmy always wanted me to drive. He had no escape when he was riding with me, and I took advantage of the opportunity to share my testimony of salvation, healing and deliverance with him.

During Christmas I hosted a party that one of the bank's executives gave for his employees. One of the employees, who happened to be a Muslim, refused the food I offered, explaining that he was feeling very sick and could not eat. When I asked if I could pray for him, he readily consented. We went into another room for privacy and I quoted healing Scriptures to him and prayed for his healing, believing that God would respond according to Psalm 107:20: "He sent His word and healed them." The employee went back to the party and I returned to my hosting duties. When I returned to the room with more food and refreshments, he was eating heartily and enjoying the festivities. He thanked me for praying for him and testified that he was completely healed.

Our catering team was small, allowing us to get to know each other and form close relationships. They knew my Christian convictions and respected me for them. Sometimes they would tease me in a good-natured way. For example, if a cold or some other illness threatened me, I would not receive it. Instead of saying, "I have a cold," I would say "I'm fighting a cold." So if I had the sniffles, the others would say, "Rosie is in a fight!"

There were many opportunities for me to give a positive witness and words of encouragement to my coworkers, without being overbearing. I had a particular compassion for our chef, Brad. He was an alcoholic, and I shared with him about how the Lord saved me and delivered me out of alcoholism, and I gave him books that would inspire and direct him. Everyone marveled at the changes that gradually took place in his life.

I had my first experience with a California earthquake one morning as I was getting ready to go to work. I felt an irresistible and urgent prompting to pray for protection, not just for myself, but also for people generally. I had been praying for about five minutes when the house began to shake violently. I recognized immediately what was happening, so I continued praying, only more fervently. I didn't know until later the severity of the earthquake, and I know that angels were protecting my property and me. A quick inspection of my house after the tremors ceased revealed no apparent damage to the structure, so I went on to work. There had been extensive damage, and I arrived to find that everyone had evacuated the building. My team was gathered together a safe distance away, praying. God had certainly got their attention! They were very glad to see me, and exclaimed, "Rose, we wouldn't have been nearly as scared if you had been here. We know that God would protect you."

During the time that I was working for the catering company, I developed severe pain in both my feet, particularly the right foot. I attributed it to a combination of stress from being on my feet so much, a slight birth deformity in my foot, and plantar warts. Any of those problems could be the source of my discomfort, but it soon became apparent that something more serious was causing my pain. Alice and I prayed, and she felt that I should take advantage of the company's excellent medical insurance and consult a podiatrist, which I did. My specialist was Dr. Berry, a Jewish doctor who had the reputation of being one of the finest podiatrists in the area.

Dr. Berry gave both my feet a thorough examination and declared that he was somewhat baffled by what he found. He had never seen a case quite like mine, and he said that I had the feet of a woman 70 years old. He would definitely have to perform surgery on my right foot, but first he wanted to do study my situation carefully, do research and consult other medical authorities. Finally, he scheduled the surgery, with the assistance of a team that included two other doctors. My employer granted me a six-month leave of absence to recuperate.

The surgery lasted several hours, much longer and more complicated than Dr. Berry anticipated. It seems that I had a tumor in my foot that was causing most of the pain I was experiencing. Dr. Berry also told me that they were not able to do everything that needed to be corrected, and that further surgery would be necessary. When I responded that the Lord would take care of me, the doctor looked at me with understanding and softly remarked, "I believe He will, because I know Him too."

Not long after my surgery, Dr. Berry ordered further x-rays to see how my foot was progressing. When he put the first picture on the screen, he looked at it and exclaimed, "How can this be?" He said nothing more while he studied the picture intently. Then he said, more to himself than to the nurse or me, "This is impossible; it must be God."

What the medical team had not been able to do, God did. Dr. Berry confessed that he had witnessed an undeniable miracle. During the time of my recuperation he asked me many questions about my relationship with God and about His miracle-working power. We became close friends, and I had such favor with him that he waived the portion of my bill that the insurance did not cover and for which I was responsible, and it was no small amount.

I had a severe allergic reaction to the antibiotics prescribed for me to guard against infection. I experienced fever and violent vomiting. As if that were not enough to endure, I also developed a staff infection in my right foot. The pain the most excruciating that I had ever experienced, and it felt like a flaming sword piercing my foot. After a sleepless night I called Dr. Berry, who ordered me to come to his medical office immediately. My foot was so painful and swollen and I was so weak that I could not even walk. A friend came for me very early in the morning and drove me to the clinic.

The doctor was quite alarmed when he removed the bandages and saw the condition of my foot. It was full of infection and terribly discolored. He took immediate action to counteract the infection and reduce the swelling. He changed my medication, making certain that I especially understood to follow his instructions about taking the powerful pain pills he gave to me. I took one in his office, but that was the last one I needed. In response to the doctor's treatment and the prayers of concerned people from my church, the Lord began the healing process at once. When I returned for a check-up later in the week, I returned the full bottle of pain pills to Dr. Berry, explaining that God had taken all the pain away. He was amazed that the only pill I had taken was the one he gave me in his office, but I gave all the glory to God.

For several weeks my foot was in a cast, so I could not wear shoes and could walk only with the help of crutches. Finally, the foot was healed enough to remove the cast, and I could wear loose tennis shoes and walk with a cane. It was then that Dr. Berry operated on my left foot, a procedure that was far less complicated than the first surgery. Once more, I had only one pain pill, and the day after the surgery I was ready to go home. The doctor examined my foot and remarked, "Rose, I just can't figure you out. You've got something my other patients don't have." I took that as an opportunity to give another witness to the goodness and greatness of God.

Several weeks after my latest surgery, I was still using a cane to assist me in walking, and I could not yet wear proper footwear. Karen, a friend from church, asked me to go with her to a Benny Hinn meeting in Palm Springs. The power of the Holy Spirit fell upon the service, and Benny began to call out healings as the Spirit directed him. At one point he announced that there was a lady with a cane who was being healed and that she should come to the platform.

I knew that word was for me, so I made my way through the crowd to the platform. While Benny continued to minister to others, I felt a pleasant heat in my heart, and I knew that it was the touch of God and that He was healing my heart. Finally, Benny came to me and said that God had healed me and that I would no longer need the cane. Having made that proclamation, he threw the cane away and touched me. The power of God hit me and I went out in the Spirit and began to laugh uproariously. After a while, Benny told the crowd, "This lady is having her own revival!" Laughter swept over the crowd. When I got to my feet, I discovered that I could walk normally, with no limp or discomfort. I no longer needed the cane, but I asked for it back. I had borrowed it, and I had to return it to its owner. I claimed for my own the blessing that Moses pronounced upon Asher: "Your shoes shall be iron and brass; as your days, so shall your strength be (Deut. 33:25).

Dr. Berry was in his mid-forties and had never married. At first his interest in me was only the professional relationship of a doctor and his patient. Gradually, however, our relationship reached a spiritual level. He saw the love of God in me and was enamored by the obvious work of God in my life. He began to take me to the finest restaurants for dinner, where we enjoyed gourmet meals that I couldn't even pronounce. He always ordered a plate for me to take home, because he said I needed to gain weight. Dr. Berry was full of questions concerning the Bible and my walk with the Lord, and he could not hear enough about my faith. The time we spent together was wonderful, and I felt that he was growing in his own relationship with the Lord.

Our relationship took an unwelcome turn when the doctor called one day to invite me on a different kind of date. This time we would have dinner as usual, but it would be at the most luxurious hotel in Beverly Hills. Afterwards, we would spend the night in a suite at the hotel. I hesitated only a split second before responding. If I had waited longer, I might have acceded, or at least I would have opened the way for a stern battle. After all, this highly successful man had been very kind to me, and I was indebted to him for my health. Not only that, but he was very handsome and most women would consider him to be quite a catch.

After that split second, I said, "Dr. Berry, I'm flattered that you should make such an offer. I have thoroughly enjoyed the time we have spent together, and I am deeply grateful for all that you have done for me, but to agree to what you are suggesting would mean betraying my Lord. I owe more to Him than I owe to you, and faithfulness to Him means far more to me than a night of pleasure with you. I will not give myself to any man outside of marriage."

I seriously doubt that any other woman had refused such a proposal from him, and for a while he was speechless. Then he continued his attempt to persuade me. Finally, he accepted my refusal and expressed his understanding and his respect for me. His offer was a severe test, and only by the strength of the Holy Spirit did I overcome it, because I had a strong attraction to the doctor and deep feelings for him. I began to pray that the Lord would take all those feelings away.

The recovery time from my surgeries was a profitable time of spiritual growth for me. I was able to spend a great deal of time communing with the Lord in prayer, praise and Bible study, and I was able to minister to many people from all walks of life. I also learned much more about ministry through attending meetings and listening to God's prophets.

During this time my mentor, Alice, sensed that the Lord was leading us to start attending the large, historic Hollywood Presbyterian Church, where the famous preacher Dr. Lloyd John Ogilvie was the pastor. There we were able to lead small group meetings, where the Lord dramatically used me in bringing salvation, healing and deliverance to many people. Many great servants of God ministered at Hollywood Presbyterian. One of the greatest meetings was a healing service led by Evangelist Mario Murillo. I witnessed many undeniable miracles, but the greatest blessing was to sit under the anointing of God.

Another person who was influential in my ministerial growth was a former witch doctor from Ghana who had been delivered from the occult and who graduated from Morris Cerullo's school of ministry. This man was mightily used of God to bring deliverance to people from generational curses, and I learned much from his ministry at Hollywood Presbyterian

Church about combating witchcraft.

On one occasion we attended a big gospel concert at MacArthur Park, featuring many prominent Christian singers. We had many opportunities to pray with and minister to people during this festival. Two experiences particularly stand out. I noticed a woman who appeared to be praying for a forlorn looking man, but something didn't seem to be right about the scene. My suspicions were confirmed when I overheard what the woman was saying, because the spirit by which she was supposedly praying was not the Holy Spirit. She was definitely of the occult. I intervened and asked the man what his problem was. He responded that he desperately wanted to be free from alcoholism. Immediately I commanded the spirit of alcoholism to release him, and two things happened. First, as I invoked the name of Jesus, the woman with the spirit of witchcraft turned and ran away as quickly as she could. At the same time, the man was totally freed and began to praise God. I shared with him about my own deliverance from alcoholism and gave him some Scriptures that would help him. We prayed with him and encouraged him to become active in a Bible-believing church.

At one point during the concert my friend and I were enjoying the music, when suddenly I heard a woman's voice call my name, "Rose Marie!" I turned to see who had shouted my name, but I could find no one who appeared to have done so. Then I saw a wretched looking old man, and I felt a drawing to him. He was a homeless alcoholic who walked among the crowd hoping for a handout or some food. We ministered to him spiritually and led him to the Lord. Then we blessed him with physical food. After I got home several hours later, I distinctly heard in my spirit, concerning that man, "Today he is with Me in Paradise." I knew then that the voice calling my name was an angel sent on assignment from God, because that man needed to be saved before he died.

Almost every day the Lord brought me into contact with all kinds of interesting people who needed spiritual help. As the Bible teaches, God orders every step when we want to do His work (see Psalm 37:23). One day at a prayer meeting I met two German ladies, Dorothy and Gabriella. Both were professing Christians, and both expressed the desire to serve God. However, they were like the Jews of the first century, who had "a zeal for God, but not according to knowledge" (Rom. 10:2). These ladies had been totally deceived by New Age doctrines, and as a result they had been targeted by Satan's strategies. I began to teach them, and the more they progressed in the truth, the more spiritual warfare they encountered.

Not long after I met Dorothy and Gabriella, I received a frantic phone call from Dorothy. Her friend was undergoing a vicious attack from the enemy, experiencing paranoia, pain and sickness, and she could not speak a word. I immediately recognized that this was the tormenting activity of a spirit of witchcraft, so I used the authority of the name of Jesus and the word of God in commanding the evil spirit to release Gabriella. This incident was tangible evidence to the two ladies of the danger of unbiblical teachings, however attractive they may be, and the resultant victory convinced them of the power that true believers have in spiritual warfare. They became mighty warriors in the kingdom of God.

During my recovery period I became a good friend and a prayer partner with a Christian realtor named Rosie, who was originally from the Philippines. Both of us were going through trying times, so we prayed for and encouraged each other. I prayed with her for many needs, but especially for her property listings, that they would sell rapidly at the best prices and that she would receive increased commissions. As for me, I was having a terrific financial struggle. I was no longer receiving a disability check, and I still could not work. My savings were depleted, and I had no funds for rent, utilities and other bills. My only resource was

Philippians 4:19: "My God shall supply all your need according to His riches in glory by Christ Jesus."

One of the most common ways that God supplies our needs is through human instrumentality. When I was at my lowest point of desperation, Rosie came to see me, flushed with excitement. "I just made a great sale!" she exclaimed, "and I know it was in response to our prayers. God told me to share my commission with you, so I want to give you $1,000.00." The Lord also sent others to help me.

I really did need a car, so I shared that need with another prayer partner, Shantel. As we were praying, she suddenly stopped and told me that the Lord had shown her that a car was reserved for me and that it would be presented as a gift to me. I gladly received that word! Over the next few days I stood in faith and praised God for the car that had been given to me. Jesus taught us to have faith in God and "whatever things you ask when you pray, believe that you have received them, and you will have them" (Mark 11:22-24). It doesn't take much faith to believe that you have something when you've got it, but to believe that you have it when you don't even see it is real faith.

One day Rosie brought her sister Maggie to my house so we could all pray together. This was the first time that I had met Maggie. One of her concerns was the sale of her car, a silver Ford sport coupe. Although it was in great condition with low mileage, she had been unable to interest anybody in buying it. It sounded very much like she was giving me a sales spiel, trying to get me to buy the car. Surely she didn't know my financial situation, and besides, I was believing God for the gift of a car.

A few days later, Maggie showed up at my door and asked me to come outside. I stepped out the door and saw in the driveway a silver Ford sport coupe with a big red bow tied around it. "This is yours," she said. "God told me to give it to you." It's a biblical principle that you can't out give God. He blessed Maggie with a brand new car, a gift from her husband.

With the gift of a car, I could now be more independent and go job-hunting more easily. I was already three months behind in my rent, and I was in dire need of a job. Of course, I searched the want ads and used every avenue possible, but I was particularly drawn to hotels. So strong was the feeling that I was to work in a hotel, I took a course in hotel management and operations. Soon after I completed the course, I obtained a job at the stately Chesterfield Hotel on Olympic Boulevard in West Los Angeles. Unfortunately, the job was only part time, which meant, of course, that I would not receive a full salary, still making it difficult to cover my bills.

In retrospect, I believe that God allowed only part-time work, because I had not fully recovered my surgery on my feet. I certainly did not need to be on my feet for hours at a time with no rest. However, the only concern I had at the time was my financial need, and I began to slip into despair and depression. Thank God, I recognized what was happening and I began to praise God. The surest antidote to depression is praise, and I did a lot of it. I stood steadfastly on the word of God, particularly Philippians 4:19, and thanked God for meeting my needs. The apartment manager wasn't impressed at all. In fact, he was quite angry and threatened eviction if the rent wasn't paid that month. On July

3, 1990, I received from an unknown source enough money to cover all my overdue bills, including the rent, and had money left over. I never discovered who my benefactor was, but God knows.

God gave me favor with my supervisors at the Chesterfield, and they began to find work for me to prolong my hours. Within weeks I was promoted to the position of assistant manager of the hotel restaurant, and I was training other people. One day, my immediate supervisor, Amy, called me aside to talk to me. We went into the bar, which was deserted at that early hour, for privacy. She got right to the point. "Rose," she said, "there are reports that you are talking about God and your faith a great deal." I responded that I witnessed only on my breaks and before and after work, and then only to people who were receptive, mostly the homosexual workers. Then I proceeded to share with her how God had delivered me from my former lifestyle and had completely changed my life. As I spoke of the love and grace of God, the presence of the Holy Spirit filled the atmosphere of the bar, and Amy began to cry, particularly when I told her how I was freed from severe alcoholism.

Not long after this conversation, Amy came to me again, and once more we visited to bar to talk. She told me that her mother was a chronic alcoholic and asked me to pray for her deliverance. We had a time of fruitful prayer, after which Amy related to me some things pertaining to her personal life. Things were exactly right between her and her husband, who was an executive in the hotel and a closet alcoholic.

One day Amy didn't show up for work, and I asked about her. What I learned was a tragedy brought on by the abuse of alcohol. Amy's husband had gone into an alcoholic rage and had cut off their child's hand. The police had arrested him and charged him. At that moment he was in jail. I thanked the Lord that I had been able to sow the word of God into Amy's life and that I would have further opportunities to minister to her during this time of extreme trial.

One evening in 1990 I served a beautiful dark-haired woman and her gorgeous blonde daughter, who appeared to be about ten or eleven years old. The restaurant wasn't too busy, since it was still early, so I had the opportunity to engage this lovely pair in conversation. They introduced themselves as Javetta Saunders and her daughter Rachel, and they were from a little town in the panhandle of Florida called Bonifay. They were in Los Angeles to meet with a singer named Beau Williams. They explained that Beau was the 1984 winner of the national television program *Star Search*, and that he had gone on to pursue a star-studded career. He had many hit recordings and had been nominated for several Grammy Awards. In 1989 he won a Dove Award for the Song of the Year, *Wonderful*. He was a regular on Christian television networks, including TBN, based in Costa Mesa, California.

Rachel was also a seasoned vocalist and had been performing publically since she was five years old. She had opened for many noted stars, such as Mel Tillis, Pat Boone and others, and she was a veteran television performer. She and Beau had recorded together a song called *They Call It Love*, written by the brilliant Nashville composer Ben Peters. They were in Los Angeles for some photo sessions and other promotional activities. I was excited to meet such interesting people and to share together our common faith. Javetta and I agreed that this meeting was by divine appointment.

A couple of days later, just before Javetta and Rachel returned to Florida, they met Beau for a late lunch, and I was their server. It was wonderful to share our experiences with the Lord, and Beau asked if we could all pray. His wife Elvina was soon due to give birth to their fourth child. I told them that I would be off from work in just a few minutes and that I would meet them in the bar. Javetta raised her eyebrows as though to question a bar as the best place to have a prayer meeting, and she declared that she had never been to a bar. I assured her that it was quite safe and the most private place to pray, because no one would be there at that hour. So we went to the bar.

As we prayed, the Lord revealed to me that the baby born to Beau and Elvina would be a girl and that she would sing for the Lord. Remember that this was before sonograms were readily available. Beau wasn't too thrilled about my announcement, and he thought that I was speaking in the flesh and not in the Spirit. A few weeks later I was watching TBN, and Paul Crouch announced that Beau Williams and his wife had just had a baby girl. They named the baby Janetta, changing one letter of Javetta's name.

Javetta and I exchanged telephone numbers and began a weekly communication. I did not know at the time how significant this meeting would become, but God was putting into motion events and relationships that would change the direction of my life. He is the master planner, and Jeremiah 29:11 tells us, "I know the thoughts that I think toward you, says the Lord, thoughts of peace and not of evil, to give you a future and a hope."

As though to confirm the fact that our meeting was arranged by divine appointment, Javetta later told me that she and Rachel were not even supposed to be staying at the Chesterfield. Her reservation was at a different hotel, but the cab driver that picked them up at the airport brought them to the Chesterfield by mistake. Javetta did not realize that they were at the wrong hotel until she tried to check in. The desk clerk apologized for the cab driver's mistake and offered Javetta a room at the same price that she would have paid at the other hotel. It made no sense to load the luggage in another cab and go to the other place, so she agreed. She had no way of knowing at that time that God had directed the whole scene.

Over the next few weeks following our meeting, Javetta and I became close friends, sometimes talking for an hour or more over the telephone. Mostly we shared favorite Scriptures and prayed for prayer requests that we expressed to each other.

Javetta is the most talented and anointed pianist I have ever heard. She can play anything, and the gift is God-given, discovered when she was five years old. She never had a music lesson in her life. She is also an accomplished singer and songwriter, and God has inspired her to write many wonderful songs. One day she called and asked me to pray with her about a song she had just written, called *Saying Yes to Life*. It was a positive approach to dealing with the drug problem, encouraging young people to say yes to life and no to drugs. She reported that for quite a while she had felt that God was leading her and Rachel to become involved with anti-drug programs, and this song was the first step. She was convinced that God would use the song in a powerful way. We agreed together in fervent prayer, and we believed that God would fulfill the promise that Jesus gave in Mark 11:24, which I quoted earlier. It was several weeks before we saw results, but we remained steadfast in our faith.

In December of 1990 I received a call from Javetta informing me that *The 700 Club* had invited Rachel, who was only eleven years old, to emcee their Christmas special. They were understandably excited about this opportunity, and Javetta wanted me to share in their experience. She offered to pay my airfare if I would meet them in Virginia Beach and then go with them to Florida to visit their family for a few days. It took me every bit of two seconds to give a positive response. First, however, I had to get permission from my supervisor at the hotel to take a few days off, and that might be very difficult during the busy Christmas season. Javetta and I prayed, and my boss reluctantly granted me an eight-day leave.

The trip would provide me with the most enjoyable time I had in years. It was a tremendous blessing for me to be at the headquarters of CBN, most especially because it was while viewing *The 700 Club* that I prayed to be saved. Just as much a blessing was my visit with Javetta and her family in Bonifay, Florida. On Sunday morning I attended First Assembly of God, where Javetta was actively involved in the music ministry. There the Lord used me On Sunday night during my visit to Florida, we attended a rural church near Bonifay. I did not know until we arrived that I was to be the speaker at the service. I was totally unprepared, but the Bible tells us, "Preach the word! Be ready in season and out of season" (2 Tim. 4:2). As I began to share what God had done for me, the anointing of the Holy Spirit came upon me to minister in power with prophecy and words of knowledge. It was a life-changing evening for several people.

On my return to Los Angeles, I had to change planes in Atlanta. While waiting for my flight I ate a hamburger in one of the airport food courts. About an hour into the flight, I became very ill with severe stomach cramps and bloating. My entire body was assaulted by waves of pain, and my head felt like it was being squeezed in a vise. I knew that I was suffering from food poisoning, but the flight attendant told me that they were not allowed to give me any medication. I began praying and rebuking the sickness that had invaded my body, and the Holy Spirit reminded me of the promise of Jesus in Mark 16:18 that we would not be harmed by any deadly thing that we might inadvertently drink. I figured that promise also included anything that we might eat, so I applied the word to my situation. I walked off the plane in Los Angeles without a trace of pain. Satan had tried to steal the blessings that I received from my unforgettable trip to Virginia and Florida, but God counteracted his attack with a miraculous healing and filled me with joy and peace.

On the evening of March 1, 1991, Javetta called me in a state of excitement. She related how as she was still sleeping early that morning, an audible voice spoke to her with the words, "In three weeks!" She felt in her spirit that this announcement had something to do with her anti-drug song, *"Saying Yes to Life,"* because she had been praying about it. By her description, we both agreed that an angel had been sent to her with a special delivery message.

Exactly three weeks later, on March 21, Javetta called again with the news that the administrative assistant to Governor Lawton Childs of

Florida had just contacted her with an invitation for Rachel to perform at an upcoming event at the capitol. She accepted immediately, assured that the invitation was an answer to prayer and that God was opening a major door.

On the day of Rachel's performance, God arranged an unscheduled private meeting with the governor. He ignored the protests of his aides that he was pressed for time and chatted with Javetta and Rachel. He expressed a keen interest in *Saying Yes to Life* and asked Rachel to sing it for him. After she finished, Javetta presented him with a copy of the published sheet music. A few days later, Javetta received communication from the governor's office, informing her that Governor Childs had officially endorsed the song as part of the drug education program for the school children of Florida. Furthermore, he had named Rachel a role model for the school children.

God had answered our prayers, but according to Ephesians 3:20, He is "able to do exceedingly abundantly above all that we ask or think," so He did just that. One of Florida's county judges secured a grant to film a video of *Saying Yes to Life*, featuring Rachel and a cast of school children. The video was produced as a public service announcement, and it was soon being televised across the nation.

The video attracted the attention of the sponsors of the Angel Awards, who honored it with a Gold Angel Award. In addition, they invited Rachel to be one of the presenters at the awards program, held at the luxurious Beverly Wilshire Hotel. Javetta again favored me by inviting me to be their guest at the event. At the press conference preceding the program, I was thrilled to meet many of my favorite celebrities, including Roy Rogers and Dale Evans and Donna Douglas, who portrayed Elly May Clampett on *The Beverly Hillbillies*. Many other well-known stars were in attendance, and I could hardly believe that I was part of such a group.

As I look back, I am more convinced than ever that God ordained the meeting of Javetta Saunders and me. As a result of that first encounter, God redirected the steps of my life's journey.

For most of the time I had spent in Los Angeles, my close friend Alice had been my spiritual mentor, as well as my guide in the practical areas of my life. Therefore, I had a mixed reaction when she told me that she was moving to Tampa, Florida, to be involved in a ministry there. I was glad for her to be a vital part of God's work wherever He might take her, but I was sad that she would no longer be near me. However, God had brought many other friends into my life, and He led me to become part of another church. This church had a vibrant prophetic ministry that was televised throughout Southern California, and I felt a genuine spiritual sanctuary there. During one service, a guest minister called me out and gave a prophecy that I would be moving to the Eastern part of the United States, and that I would serve the Lord in a ministry there and that I would meet my mate. That word, at least the part about moving, was a confirmation to me, because the Lord had already been dealing with me about a shifting in my life. As far as the other part was concerned, I was content to wait on the Lord.

On April 29, 1992, a jury acquitted four police officers, three white and one Hispanic, of beating a black driver, Rodney King, after a high-speed chase. Immediately, violent riots broke out in Los Angeles, with widespread looting, arson, assault and murder. White motorists were pulled from their cars and beaten by enraged mobs, and in some areas a new fire broke out every minute. During the six days following the verdict, 53 people were killed and thousands more were injured. Property damage was over a billion dollars, including 1,100 buildings destroyed by fire. Only a rigid curfew enforced by a coalition of the Los Angeles Police Department, the California National Guard, and the United States Army and Marines finally quelled the riots.

When the riots broke out, the management of the Chesterfield Hotel warned its employees of the danger of being on the streets and gave them the option of staying at the hotel. I did not take the warning seriously, so I went home to take care of some matters there. The next morning I was stopped at a traffic light while I was driving to work. It was not yet six o'clock in the morning, but already people were gathering in groups on the streets. While I was held up at the light, a man swinging a big club came running toward me. The anger on his face left no doubt about what he intended. At the same time, other rioters moved into the street to cut off my way of escape. I feared for my life and began to call on the Lord to protect me. The man with the club stopped two feet from my car, and the crowd converging in front of me jumped aside as I sped away. I could only praise God for fulfilling Psalm 91, where He promised protection from all evil.

During the riots, a large group of German tourists were stranded at the hotel, giving me a great opportunity to interact with them. I served as their translator, and they were full of questions. When one of them asked me why I was so happy, I had an open door to share the love of God. Nobody but the Germans could understand what I was saying, so I could give an unrestrained witness.

I already had much favor with the homosexual employees of the hotel, but during the riots I gained new respect from them. They were careful to guard their language around me, and we developed a congenial relationship. One day one of the cooks sought me out to pray for his arm, which he had painfully injured in a fall. During the riots, the bar was more crowded than usual, so we found a quiet place in the rear of the kitchen, where I prayed for him. The next day he was swinging his arm and testifying to everyone that he had experienced a miracle of healing.

Everything returned to normal after the riots ended. One morning as I was driving to work and praying for the day's activities, my car suddenly accelerated on its own. I applied the brakes to slow down, but they didn't work. I tried to turn off the ignition, but I couldn't. As the car kept accelerating faster and faster, I was praying faster and faster to match it. A traffic light ahead of me was red, and I raced through it, passing a patrol car with two policemen in it. They were either looking in the opposite direction, or an angel blinded them momentarily. For whatever reason, they didn't pursue me. I praised God, because there was no way I could have stopped, and I didn't want another Rodney King incident.

I was praying fervently in the Spirit and quoting Scripture concerning God's protection, especially Isaiah 54:17, which declares that no weapon formed against me would prosper. Finally, I managed to work the gearshift into neutral and coasted into a parking lot. The motor was still racing, but I could not turn off the ignition. I got out of the car, shaking with fear. Then I became angry and started rebuking the devil and whatever evil spirits were assigned to this mission of destruction, using the authority of the name of Jesus and the word of God. Some people going into places of business were looking at me strangely, and I'm sure they thought I had done some early drinking, or maybe I had been at it all night. I got back into the car and started talking to the vehicle, commanding it to calm down and operate normally, like it was supposed to do. I turned the ignition off. It worked! I had a praise session in the car, thanking God for His protection and praising Him in advance that the car would run smoothly. I turned the key to start the engine. It purred like a Singer sewing machine! I drove on to work without further incidence, and I had no similar problems with the car. I had another testimony to share, and everyone heard it before the day was over.

In the spring of 1992 at Javetta's invitation, I went to Florida again, this time to Orlando, where Rachel was competing in a beauty pageant. After the pageant was over, we visited WACX-TV, or as it was more popularly known, SuperChannel 55. Javetta's sister and brother-in-law, Freeda and Claud Bowers, were founders and head of this powerful Christian television station that had an audience of several million. They invited me to appear as a special guest on one of their live prime-time programs, informing me that as many as five million people would be watching. Before I appeared, Javetta sang a song entitled *There's a Miracle in the Making*, not realizing that the song was prophetic of what would happen during the program. As Claud interviewed me and asked me to share about how God had delivered me out of a life of prostitution, alcoholism and the occult, a powerful anointing for deliverance came upon me. Even as I was speaking, the telephones began ringing, as people were calling for prayer and to testify of salvation and deliverance from all kinds of bondage, including drugs, alcoholism and sexual sins. I learned later that the phones were still ringing hours later.

Over the next few months, Javetta and I were in contact by telephone almost daily, praying over prayer requests from each other and from others. We saw many needs met as we stood on the promise of Jesus: "If two of you agree on earth concerning anything that they ask, it will be done for them by My Father in heaven" (Matt. 18:19).

One prayer request came from Javetta's son, Shannon, that he might kill a deer. Though some might think such a request was trite or unseemly, it was important to him, because he had never killed a deer, although he had been hunting many times. A few days after we prayed, Javetta called to report that Shannon had killed his first deer.

That was not the only prayer concerning Shannon that God answered. He was a very popular teenager, and he liked to party with other young people of questionable character, particularly on weekends. He was facing some typical teenage challenges, and Javetta carried a heavy burden for him. Consequently, we spent many hours praying for him. One night as we were praying, the Lord gave me a vision of Shannon dressed in a black robe. I had no idea what it meant, but Javetta and I both felt that it was a positive sign from God and that its significance would become clear.

It wasn't long before we saw a dramatic change in Shannon. He rededicated his life to the Lord and began to get serious about his studies, and he saw extraordinary improvement in his grades. After graduating from high school, he first attended a local community college and then studied pre-law at Auburn University. Before entering law school, he married Amy, a lovely young lady he met in college. Today he is one of the most successful trial lawyers in Northwest Florida and heads his own large law firm. He and Amy have two beautiful children. Javetta and I feel that the vision I had of Shannon dressed in a black robe represents law, but that it is only partly fulfilled. Is a judgeship or something even greater in his future?

We also prayed diligently for Javetta's other children, her older son,

Steven, and her daughter, Rachel, that they would always be committed to God's will and that they would go through only the doors that He opened for them. Steven graduated from four different universities, with B.A., M.A. and PhD degrees in psychology. He has a successful counseling practice and heads several clinics, while also serving as an adjunct on the faculty of Central Florida University. He is happily married with two fine boys.

Following her graduation with high honors from Oral Roberts University, Rachel served as a public relations official in the administration of Governor Jeb Bush of Florida. She then moved to Nashville to pursue a career as a Christian recording artist and songwriter. She has released two CDs, with the last one consisting entirely of her original songs. Rachel also established a successful real estate business and obtained a MBA degree. She is married to Greg Dampier, a Christian musician whom she met through her church in Nashville.

I had not forgotten the prophecy that I would move to the Eastern part of the United States, and God had been preparing me for such a move. In fact, there were many signs that He would be moving me to Florida. In spite of the certainty that God wanted me to relocate, it was still difficult for me to think about leaving Los Angeles. It had been my adopted home for sixteen years, and I loved Southern California, especially for its climate. It didn't help to think of the hot and humid atmosphere to which I would be going. However, when God overcame my indecision about the time that I should leave and gave me the release to resign my job, I felt immediate peace and joy. After all, God promises that we "shall go out with joy, and be led out with peace" (Isa. 55:12).

I did not want to leave undone some things that I needed to accomplish before leaving Los Angeles. For several years I had been having my nails done at the same parlor, so I went there for the last time.

This time, however, I made certain that the Buddhist workers clearly understood the way to be saved. Every one of them accepted Jesus Christ as their Savior that day, and I left with a complimentary nail job.

For sixteen years I had lived in the same apartment complex, and I had faithfully witnessed to the managers and their families and to other residents. Shortly before I left, I invited the manager and his family and all the friends of their children to a pizza party. The special guest was Jesus, and I introduced Him to everyone present. All the children asked Him to come into their hearts.

My pastor, Danny Fernandez, and his wife led the church in a commissioning service, during which they released me for ministry with their prayers and with a financial gift. At a home service I received a prophetic word about my future. The message was that I would minister to many, many people, even in high places.

I had finally tied up all the loose ends, and I was leaving nothing behind. I even gave my car to a friend, a lady from Germany who helped me in my preparation to leave. I left Los Angeles on Tuesday, September 1, 1992. It was truly a bold step of faith for me to leave behind the security that I had known for so long, but I also knew that God could not give me something else if I refused to let go of what I had.

I arrived in Panama City, Florida, where Javetta was waiting for me at the airport. She drove me to Bonifay, her hometown of about 4,000 people. There I settled into a lovely furnished apartment owned by a local pastor and his wife. I took part in many Christian meetings in the area, and became part of a small full gospel church located just outside the city. There I was the recipient of many blessings.

Javetta and I returned to Orlando to take part in SuperChannel 55's telethon. She ministered in song and word, and I had the great blessing of praying with people who called during the telecast, ministering to their needs and leading many to salvation. Donna Douglas was also there, and her testimony brought such a response that all the phones were tied up, and people had to wait to get through. The next day, Donna ministered at a singles conference at the Orlando Christian Center, where Benny Hinn was pastor at the time. She asked me to accompany her and to take part in the ministry, which I did and with great results.

118

The brief time that I had been in Bonifay was filled with so many exciting events that I wondered what could happen next. I could only praise God that He led me there and opened so many doors for me to serve Him and to make so many new friends. I was finding more and more opportunities to teach people from the word of God and from my own experiences, particularly in the area of spiritual warfare. Just after Javetta and I returned from Orlando, I was meditating on the goodness of God and praising Him, when suddenly the words of Isaiah 52:7 appeared before me, as though the Holy Spirit projected them before the eyes of my spiritual understanding: "How beautiful upon the mountains are the feet of him who brings good news, who proclaims peace, who brings glad tidings of good things, who proclaims salvation." I could only humbly bow before the Lord that I could be a messenger to proclaim such good news.

One afternoon two of my new friends dropped in unexpectedly to visit. We enjoyed a wonderful conversation and then we prayed together. While we were praying, the Lord gave me a picture of a boat about to capsize, and I felt that we urgently needed to pray protection for the occupants of the boat. I did not know that the husbands of the ladies visiting me were out fishing. The next day one of the ladies reported to me that the boat the men were in was sinking, and there was not another boat in sight. Miraculously, another boat appeared out of nowhere, and the men were rescued. We praised God for His love and for using me as an intercessor.

One night I had a very vivid dream that I knew was from God and that it meant something significant in my future. In the dream I saw a man walking down a long hallway with many doors on both sides. He did not pause as he walked past the doors, until suddenly he stopped and looked back. Somehow I had caught his attention, and when he turned I sensed a warm spirit in him and I felt love flowing out of him. He walked back to the last room and put a key in the door and opened it. I called my friend and mentor, Alice, to relate the dream to her. She responded, "That dream is from God, and the man will come into your life very soon."

The dream actually came to pass sooner than I expected. I attended a home prayer meeting, at which the Holy Spirit gave many visible evidences of His presence. At one point the Spirit gave me a prophecy to speak concerning a man named Bill, whom I had never met. Bill began to weep, because the prophecy confirmed to him that he would pick up the calling that his father never fulfilled. The Lord had already impressed this fact upon him, and he had been licensed to preach, although he was not ordained.

After the prayer meeting concluded, Bill and his cousin offered to drive me home. When we reached my house, we sat in the car for a while to talk. Bill gave me his business card and asked me to call him when I returned from a trip that I had planned.

A week later, upon my return, I called Bill. He had been to the dentist that day to have a tooth extracted, and he could not stop the bleeding. I prayed and spoke over him the words of Ezekiel 16:6: "And when I passed by you and saw you struggling in your own blood, I said to you in your blood, 'Live!' Yes, I said to you in your blood, 'Live!'" There was a pause, and then with excitement he exclaimed that the bleeding had stopped.

After that initial conversation, Bill and I visited on the telephone more frequently. We soon became closely acquainted and we began to go to church services together and occasionally to dinner. Our conversations were usually more about spiritual matters than things of a personal nature. One evening, however, he confided in me that he had been praying with his pastor for the past three years for a godly wife. I thought little of this disclosure until we were sitting together in a church service. I felt warmth emanating from him, and when I turned to look at him I saw that his face was aglow. Then I knew that this was the man that I had seen in my dream. Instantly, joy and love flooded my heart, and I silently whispered, "Lord, what's happening to me?"

A few days after that experience, I was in my apartment having my daily devotion time with the Lord, and in my spirit I heard Him tell me to get ready, because it won't be long. I knew what the words meant, and joy filled my heart. I was nervous as a schoolgirl, and I prayed the Lord to help me be ready. That very week Bill asked me to marry him, and truly believing that God had ordained it, I enthusiastically agreed. Our courtship was quite brief, and we married without delay. Our honeymoon was a ministry trip to South Carolina, and upon our return we began an evangelistic ministry in Northwest Florida.

Several months after our marriage, Bill told me that he had dreamed that he was going to be the pastor of a church. Two weeks later, the Church of God in Graceville, Florida, called him to be their pastor. A tremendous period of growth and a mighty outpouring of the Holy Spirit characterized our time there. Miracles took place in almost every service, with physical, emotional, spiritual and financial healings. Sometimes the power of God was so strong that people literally got drunk from the Spirit's anointing, and it seemed just like the Day of Pentecost.

One miracle in particular remains vividly fixed in my memory. A young woman who was in her seventh month of pregnancy, but the doctors had told her that the baby was brain dead and that he would be stillborn. We prayed for a miracle of healing and chose to believe the report of the Lord rather than the report of the medical authorities. When the young lady later gave birth, there were no complications and the baby was perfect.

One Sunday, men from the Teen Challenge ministry had charge of the service at our church. During the service I gave a message in tongues, followed by the interpretation. One of the men at Teen Challenge for rehab cried out, "That message is for me. That's the same voice I heard in a dream just before I entered Teen Challenge, and it confirms that I am in the right place for God to deliver me and that He will use me." That service opened the door for me to teach and minister at Teen Challenge, and God changed many lives.

In 1999 the Lord released us from the church in Graceville and we moved to another Church of God in Panama City, Florida. The pattern of ministry that we had experienced in the church we had just left continued in our new work. In a short period of time many people were saved, healed and delivered. Even a witch was saved and delivered from demonic activity.

Our tenure in Panama City was short-lived, because late in the year 2001 we relocated to Bowling Green, Kentucky, where Bill accepted a position as the administrator of a retirement home. We ministered in the chapel there and we were actively involved in an outreach ministry.

There was tremendous pressure upon us in our work in Bowling Green. We faced daily attacks against out ministry, our marriage and our personal lives. In the spring of 2002, Bill suggested that perhaps it would be less stressful if I went back to Bonifay to escape the pressure, while he remained as the administrator of the retirement home. I agreed after he assured me that it would be only a temporary arrangement, and that we would see each other for a few days at least every month.

The "temporary arrangement" soon stretched into a year, and the visits that Bill made to Bonifay became less frequent. There was always a pressing duty or some other excuse, and our lives seemed to be going in opposite directions. Things were definitely not right, and what was happening was not healthy for a marriage. I began to get paranoid, because Bill was not the same man who professed such great love for me. At the times he did get back to Bonifay, he was more like a visiting stranger. Finally, I gave him an ultimatum concerning our untenable situation. If our marriage was to survive, we were going to have to live together and minister together as a team.

Bill agreed with me and asked for time to wind up his responsibilities in Kentucky. He promised that as soon as he had things in order, he would retire and come back to Florida. I accepted his word and in hope and expectation I eagerly waited for the day of his return, so we could resume the life and ministry we once knew and enjoyed so much.

He was true to his word, and he soon returned to Florida, and we moved to a new location we had selected just outside of Chipley, Florida. We spent one night there, and the next morning he presented me with the shock of my life. Without any explanation or forewarning, he just handed me divorce papers and walked out. I was devastated beyond any anguish I had ever known before. Immediately I called Javetta and others for support. Javetta came immediately and began ministering to me and brought a great deal of comfort and strength to me.

The next few days were pivotal in my life. My heart was crushed,

124

and in my feeling of hopelessness I was vulnerable to the attacks of the enemy. I could not eat and I slept fitfully. Satan used every weapon in his arsenal to destroy me. He brought up my past life to heap shame and unworthiness on me. He beat me down with a sense of low self-esteem. He tried to place all the blame on me by telling me that I was not a loving and submissive wife, and that I was a cold, overbearing and dominating woman who criticized her husband and put him down.

Satan is a liar, but he is also relentless. There were moments when I entertained his lies, but the Holy Spirit within me rose to my defense, and I resisted the devil's challenge with the word of God. A friend called to remind me of the words of Jesus to Peter when Satan was besetting him: "I have prayed for you, that your faith should not fail" (Luke 22:31, 32). Someone else reminded me of how the brothers of Joseph sold him into slavery, and he declared that while they meant it for evil, God meant it for good (Gen. 50:20). Another one ministered to me from Zechariah 9:12: "Return to the stronghold, you prisoners of hope. Even today I declare that I will restore double to you."

I knew that God was faithful and that He would sustain me. I leaned heavily on His promise of Jeremiah 29:11: "For I know the thoughts that I think toward you, says the Lord, thoughts of peace and not of evil, to give you a future and a hope." God had plans for me, and He was not through with me yet. In the midst of my anguish I prayed the Lord to have mercy on Bill. It was a tremendous burden to me that he had forsaken God's purpose and will for his ministry.

If it had not been for the fulfillment of the promise of 1 Corinthians 10:13, I could not have survived. God promised that He would allow nothing to come against us beyond our ability to endure, and He also promised that He would provide a way of escape. That verse of Scripture was a strong anchor to me throughout the desolate weeks of broken-hearted wretchedness that I experienced. I felt that I was literally walking through the valley of the shadow of death, and only the certainty that God was with me sustained me (see Psalm 23:4).

The enemy sought to destroy me by constantly dredging up my past, trying to convince me that I was unworthy and that God was punishing me for all my past sins. Of course that was a lie, because God had forgiven me and cleansed me from all unrighteousness (1 John 1:9). My sins were nowhere in God's sight, because God had removed them from me "as far as the east is from the west" (Psalm 103:12), and he buried them in "the depths of the sea" (Micah 7:19) and He remembers them no more (Jer. 31:34; Heb. 8:12).

What the devil could not do in the spiritual realm, he tried to do in the emotional realm. He bombarded me with weapons of doubt, fear, loneliness, rejection and every other imaginable emotion of destruction.

I was in a constant battle day and night, and I was on the verge of a total breakdown. I could barely eat or sleep, and I went through the motions of daily life. Finally, one night I fell asleep from complete exhaustion, and I experienced a beautiful visitation from the Lord. I awakened during the night, sensing a strong presence next to my bed. I was not afraid, because an intense atmosphere of peace and comfort pervaded the room, and I breathed in such a beautiful sweet-scented fragrance that it was indescribable. I knew that it was the One described in Song of Solomon 2:1 as the Rose of Sharon and the Lily of the Valleys. That night I bathed in the glory of the Lord, and I received unshakeable assurance of God's promise in Isaiah 43:1, 2: "Fear not, for I have redeemed you; I have called you by your name: you are Mine. When you pass through the waters, I will be with you; and through the rivers, they shall not overflow you. When you walk through the fire, you shall not be burned, nor shall the flame scorch you."

I cried a lot that night, but this time the tears were of a different kind. I did not weep tears of sorrow; they were tears of praise and gratitude that God loved me so much. I knew that He would be my companion and that He would take care of me.

Day after day I grew stronger physically, emotionally and spiritually as God led me through a healing process. My precious sister in the Lord, Javetta Saunders, resolutely stood by me and ministered to me constantly with prayer, Scripture and genuine love. Later, another dear friend, Pearlie Noble, and her sister became faithful prayer partners with me, and they remain the same today.

I found life and hope in the word of God. Psalm 20 declared to me that God had heard me in the midst of my trouble, and that He was my defender, my helper and my strength. 2 Chronicles 26:5 instructed me that as long as I sought the Lord, He would prosper me. Scriptures such as these, along with prayer, were my mainstay, and I became more intimate with God than ever before. I grew in knowledge of Him and developed a greater love for Him. During this time I gained a deeper understanding of the needs of others and felt a more intense and genuine compassion for them.

The divorce was scheduled for mid-August, 2003, but for some inexplicable reason it was delayed. I realized later that God had caused the delay in my favor, when I learned that if I had been married for ten years I would have the benefits and legal rights to my husband's retirement. The divorce became final two months after our tenth anniversary. God is faithful to watch over His own.

I later learned some things that helped me to understand Bill's actions, especially when he remarried not long after our divorce. He had become involved with this woman even before we moved to Kentucky from Florida. That apparently was the reason he suggested that I return to Florida. I had no desire to retaliate against Bill, preferring to commit the matter to God and let Him deal with it. Vengeance is God's jurisdiction, not mine. I just wanted to forgive and go on with my own life and ministry. Not long after the divorce, Bill called me and asked forgiveness.

The succeeding weeks provided a marked contrast in the ministry that I continued to pursue and in events surrounding Bill. While many new doors of opportunity opened to me, it was evident that the favor of God had left him. People often ask me whether or not I was in God's will when I married Bill. It may seem paradoxical to say that I was, in light of what happened, but it was weak humanity that failed, not God. I had received prior notice that I would be married, in both prophecy and dream, and confirmed by the witness that I felt in my inner self. Even as I look back, I can honestly say that I was convinced that my marriage was ordained of God, but in the midst of God's will we still have the choice of rebellion. In seeking an understanding of why my husband chose to reject me, I have searched the years that we were married and had a fruitful ministry as a team, and I have examined my relationship to him as a wife. I realized that I was far from ideal and that I was not without my faults. We also faced many things that we would have to work to overcome. In spite of knowing all about my history, Bill accepted me as a new creature in Christ, righteous in Him, but I cannot know how much my pre-Christian conduct preyed on his mind. I realized that there were differences in our personalities, and certainly differences in our cultures, but we seemed to be of one mind in Christ, with common goals and motives and a common commitment. I do not condemn him for leaving me for another woman, but the only valid explanation I can suggest for the failure of our marriage is human weakness. I could choose to react with bitterness and self-pity and spend the rest of my life bemoaning the fact that I was jilted and treated unfairly. I could also choose to react in self-condemnation, beating myself down from not being the dutiful and loving wife that I should have been, and failing to meet my husband's needs. Either choice would have been an insurmountable obstacle to future growth in my life and a serious hindrance to any ministry that I might pursue, and I would have wallowed in the misery of lonely isolation. Instead, I chose to follow the path of mercy and forgiveness, both to Bill and myself, and to renew my original commitment to God to do and to be whatever He planned for me.

The Bible presents the purpose and ideal of marriage as a life-long union symbolizing Christ's perfect love for His church (Gen. 2:24; Matt. 19:4-6; Eph. 5:21-33), but in marriage as in all other areas of life, we have the choice of whether or not we fulfill God's purpose. Some churches and some denominations will not allow a divorced person to minister among them. Of course, if you had murdered your spouse, you can be forgiven, but your divorce cannot be forgiven. However, the same churches that teach God's purpose and ideal of exclusive, committed, lifelong faithfulness in marriage should also present clear and practical teaching about the duty and the way of forgiveness, because reconciliation is at the very heart of the gospel. The same God who said, "I hate divorce" (Mal. 2:16), also said through the prophet Hosea, whose wife had been blatantly immoral: "I will heal their backsliding and I will love them freely, for My anger has turned away from them" (Hos. 14:4). It is pharisaic to become more preoccupied with divorce and its grounds than with marriage and its ideals. We must see Scripture as a whole, and not isolate the topic of divorce.

My experience has taken from me a judgmental attitude toward divorced people in any proud or condemning way; it has rather led me to confess the universal taint of sin in which all of us are personally involved. It has also enabled me to share with deep compassion in the suffering of those whose marriage has failed.

As the days and weeks passed following the breakup of my marriage, I received more and more physical, emotional and spiritual strength as God's poured out His grace upon me. I began to realize more clearly the meaning of 2 Corinthians 12:9: "My grace is sufficient for you, for My strength is made perfect in weakness." It's a biblical principle that God displays His power in our lives not in **our** strength and **our** ability; it is our **weakness** and **our** inability (see 1 Cor. 1:26-29).

Many times we pray, "Lord, I could serve you so much better if you would just change my circumstances." "Change my spouse." "Move me to another position." "Take me to another town." But God can only use us and be glorified in our lives when we are weak and recognize our total dependence upon Him. The apostle Paul declared, "Therefore, most gladly I will rather glory in my infirmities that the power of Christ may rest upon me" (2 Cor. 12:9). His outlook showed me that I could have victory in the midst of my difficulties. I had just gone through the most stressful time of my life, but knowing that God was going to use that experience caused me to glory in it. So I gave a shout of victory in the midst of my distresses, and my whole viewpoint was changed.

I not only realized victory in the midst of my situation; the power of Christ became like a tent spread over me, and I lived under the shelter of that power. If I had complained and grown bitter and judgmental, I would never have known the shelter of the power of Christ and I would never have experienced the power of the risen Lord abiding on me and made available to me. I had been praying, "Lord, You just don't know the problems I'm going through. Lord, look at my situation. Look at my heartache. Lord, do something!" God answered, "My grace is sufficient for you." I could not understand all the things that happened to me, especially since I had been so faithful to the Lord. As far as I knew, I had totally surrendered everything to Him without reservation and I had served Him with my entire being. So why did this happen?

I learned that the grace of God is sufficient, no matter what the situation is. Now I walk, not in the power of my own strength or experiences, but in the certainty that in my weakness His power is perfected.

One afternoon Javetta came to my apartment for a time of fellowship and prayer. We were praying and praising God and speaking His word, when all of a sudden, I exclaimed, "An angel is here with us!" Immediately, Javetta cried out, "Rose, did you see what I just saw?" I had indeed witnessed the same phenomenon that she saw. There was the manifestation of a bright light shining on the left side of the ceiling that went across to the other side of the ceiling. I remembered the words of Psalm 103:20 that tell us that the angels, who excel in strength, hearken to the voice of the word of God and perform it. We had been praying the word of God over our needs, and angels were at work in our behalf.

I began to flow in ministry as new opportunities came from churches and home meetings, only now there was a distinct difference in the way God used me. I was an empty vessel, and God gave me a special anointing to minister to people going through depression and grief, especially from the stress of divorce. We witnessed many miracles of deliverance and rejoiced to see people set free from their bondage.

Before one service, the Lord instructed me to take along my "overseas" suitcase and told me how to use it. After I gave a teaching from the Bible on God's power to heal and deliver, I opened the suitcase and told the people to dump all their fears and problems and difficulties into it. Jesus told us in Mark 11:23 that "whoever says to this mountain (hindrances and obstacles), 'Be removed and be cast into the sea,' and does not doubt in his heart, but believes that those things he says will be done, he will have whatever he says." So we figuratively drowned all our troublesome situations and difficulties in the sea. The Lord honored our faith, and many people experienced His delivering power.

One Sunday I was driving to Marianna, Florida, to minister at a church. As I was praising the Lord and praying for the service, two beautiful white doves flew abreast of the car next to my window. I was overwhelmed and I felt the anointing of the Holy Spirit come upon me. The presence of God was mightily evidenced in the service. When I gave the altar call, seven children came forward to be saved. Three children and one adult received the baptism in the Holy Spirit and began speaking in tongues. All over the church the young people were excited and were praying for one another. I was still at the altar, praying for people. While I was praying for a seven-year-old boy, he began speaking in tongues. Then he told how the Lord had given him a vision as we were praying. He saw me in the vision under attack by the enemy, but God sent angels to protect me and I was walking in victory. At the same time, my friend and prayer partner, Pearlie Noble, had a word from the Lord for me concerning my future. She saw the word of God wrapped around me like a cloak. Some of the words were written in red, signifying the words of Jesus. So I was under the protection of the word of God and the hosts of heaven!

One night Javetta and I ministered at a lovely rural church near

134

Columbus, Georgia. She sang and I testified and preached the word. Special guests at the service were men from Valley Rescue Mission, a Christian rehab center for men addicted to drugs and alcohol, and Damascus Way, a similar institution for women. I was speaking to a congregation that consisted mostly of men and women enslaved by the chains of addiction. I could speak their language, and I felt their bondage, because I too had been in those chains, and even worse. As I spoke of the power of God to save and deliver, there was scarcely a movement as the entire congregation was captivated by the convicting power of the word of God. I laid hands on every one of those addicts and ministered to them the deliverance of God and commanded the tormenting demons in their lives to fee them. The Holy Spirit came upon each one. Some were crying; some were shouting; some were praying; some were laughing; but all were rejoicing in their liberty. It was a dramatic manifestation of the presence and power of the Holy Spirit.

About two years later, I heard a report someone who met one of the young addicts who had been in that service. The young man was now in Bible school and he was preaching the gospel and had gone on mission trips. He gave his testimony of what happened in the service when the power of God came upon him and he was completely delivered. He concluded by saying, "My life was completely turned around that night, and it will never be the same."

The Lord also gave me a burden for the nations of the world. One night I was watching a report on TBN about a Reinhart Bonnke crusade in Africa. A sea of more than a hundred thousand people were present, and tens of thousands responded to the call to receive Christ as their Savior. As I watched, God touched me with a supernatural compassion for all the people of Africa. My tears were uncontrollable, and cried and prayed for hours that Africa might be saved. Never had I experienced such a time of intercession as that.

Recently, I was watching a report about my native country of Germany taking a stand for Israel. I rejoiced at this news, and it brought back a powerful memory of something that happened several years ago in Los Angeles. I was in a church service in which a judge by the name of Eve Cohen, who was a Messianic Jew, was ministering. During the service she began praying for the nations of the world. Suddenly, she stopped and by the inspiration of the Holy Spirit, she said, "There is someone here that represents the nation of Germany. Please come forward." I went to the front and she laid hands on me and prayed for Germany, speaking forgiveness to the nation for what they did during the Holocaust. God has given me a great love for the Jewish people, and I pray daily for the nation of Israel.

Over the last few years of my personal ministry, I have been under the covering of Pastor Earlie Flowers and his wife Gloria, a wonderful couple from Northwest Florida. I have ministered in several times in the church where they serve, and the Lord has mightily blessed in various ways. In one service a prophetic anointing came upon me. One prophecy that I particularly remember concerns a couple that I had never met and about whom I knew nothing. I learned later that the husband was the pastor's nephew and that he and his wife had six children. I asked them to stand and announced to them that the Lord was going to give them a new house. When you declare something like that, you better know that you are in the Spirit! Two weeks later, a fire destroyed the house in which they were living. Only a short time later they were presented with a much larger house, free of charge. They still testify of their miracle house.

Through Pastor Flowers I met a couple that own a furniture store, which had been family operated for a long time. Once a week they conduct a Bible study and prayer meeting after hours at their store. I felt the Lord leading me to encourage them by attending the meetings and praying for their business. They were in dire financial straits and were in a battle with the IRS over back taxes. In their need they tithed their business income and trusted God to meet their needs.

One day I happened by their store and saw them moving furniture out of the building. I stopped and asked them why they were moving their inventory out of the building. They were under a fearful strain, because their hearing with the IRS was the next day, and their tax attorney gave them no hope that there would be a settlement in their favor. I felt bold faith rising up within me, and I proclaimed, "That will not be the case at all! God is on your side, so you can put the furniture back." I declared to them, "I have never seen the righteous forsaken or his seed begging for bread" (Psalm 37:25). Then I assured them that I would go home and intercede for them.

That night I engaged in major spiritual warfare and intercession. The next day I received a phone call from the couple, announcing that God had shown them great favor in the hearing and that the IRS had drastically reduced their payment by thousands of dollars. They were able to work out a payment system whereby they could make small monthly payments. God immediately began to prosper their business, and they have almost paid their debt in full.

I want to continue to "be a vessel for honor, sanctified and useful for the Master, prepared for every good work" (2 Tim. 2:21), and I want to fulfill His call on my life. Nothing has been the same in my life since I met Jesus Christ. The moment that He came into my life I became a new creation, and the old things in my life passed away. At that same moment, everything in my life became new (2 Cor. 5:17).

I like to think of the biography of every Christian as containing two volumes. The first volume, entitled *The Old You* or *The Old Life*, ended with your new birth in Christ. It's finished forever, and you need never to open it again. The second volume, entitled *The New You* or *The New Life*, began where the first volume concluded, when Christ came into your life. That volume is still being written, and you are adding to it every day. It never gets old.

That analogy certainly describes my life. I'm not proud of the first volume, which I have summarized in this book, but I know that I will never live there again. It's closed forever. I'm living in the second volume, and every day is a new experience in Christ. In this book I have also summarized that volume up to this point, but there is much more to be added, and I'll depend upon the Lord to provide the details.

I encourage those of you who are still living in Volume 1 of your biography to close it and begin Volume 2 by asking Jesus to save you, "for whoever calls on the name of the Lord shall be saved" (Rom. 10:13). You have the promise "that if you confess with your mouth the Lord Jesus and believe in your heart that God has raised Him from the dead, you will be saved" (Rom. 10:9). You can experience complete freedom in Christ.

I am a miracle. You can be one as well. If you have never been born again, I urge you to pray this prayer: "Dear God, I confess that I am a sinner, and I'm sorry for my sins. I repent and ask you to forgive me. I believe that Jesus died on the cross for my sins, and I receive salvation in His name. According to Your word, I confess Christ as my Lord, and I confess that You raised Him from the dead. I accept Jesus as my Savior and I receive Him into my heart."

The power of Jesus can break the bonds of your addiction, whatever it may be. I know. It happened to me, and I was bound with the chains of more than one addiction. If you are in such a struggle and you want to be free, there are some steps that you can follow to receive deliverance.

First, reaffirm your faith in Jesus. If you have never been born again, pray the prayer that I suggested.

Then identify and renounce all the addictions and practices that have enslaved you. The addiction may be alcoholism, drugs, pornography, tobacco, gambling, or some similar indulgence. Or it may be something that appears to be innocent in itself, such as computer or video games, but it has such a stranglehold on you that you indulge it in valuable hours that rob you of work and family. Or it may be an attitude, such as greed, jealousy, envy, pride, unforgiveness, or some other destructive characteristic. By practices I mean things associated with the occult, such as witchcraft, fortune telling, the horoscope, New Age philosophy, and the like.

Confess and repent of your involvement in these sins, renounce them and forsake them.

Forgive anybody who has offended or hurt you. Jesus said in Mark 11:25: "And whenever you stand praying, if you have anything against anyone, forgive him . . ."

Submit to the Lord's truth and power and believe in your authority in Christ. The work of demonic powers is often present in cases of addiction. In such cases, it is necessary to rebuke the evil spirits, but only if you have first renounced the addiction. Jesus has given to those who believe in Him authority over all demonic powers (Luke 10:19). Speak the word of God that applies to your situation in your rebuke, because it has great authority. The angels will help you in your battle, because they heed the voice of God's word and has to do it (Psalm. 103:20). Exercise the power that you have in Christ and command all evil activity to depart.

Walk in God's praises.

Those of you seeking to be free from any kind of sinful addiction or practice may pray a prayer on this order:

"Father your word says that I can come boldly into your throne room to obtain mercy and find grace to help in time of need (see Heb. 4:16). Therefore, I come to you boldly and declare your word over my life. I renounce all habits and practices that harass me, that entice me, that enslave me, and I forbid them to dominate my life, because I am a child of God. I confess my sins to You (name them aloud before God). I repent of all my sins. I renounce any form of the occult or idolatry in my life or in the life of my ancestors (to the best of your knowledge, identify such involvement by you or your ancestors). I forgive anyone who has ever hurt me in any way, and I let go of bitterness and resentment (name the people who have wronged you and forgive each one). I believe I am saved by the grace of God and cleansed by the blood of Jesus. I am justified, just as if I had never sinned. I am set apart unto God. Therefore, Satan has no further legal rights to my spirit, soul, mind, or body. In the name of Jesus, I bind every evil spirit in and around my life and I command you to cease your vexation and flee from me. Go in the name of Jesus! Thank you, Father, for saving and delivering me. By the power of the Holy Spirit, help me to stand on your word and walk in daily victory."

"But now having been set free from sin, and having become slaves of God, you have your fruit to holiness, and the end, everlasting life" (Rom. 6:22).

Make certain that you become part of a Bible-believing church, where you can find fellowship with and support from other Christians and grow through worship and the teaching of the Bible. Establish a time of disciplined Bible study and prayer. You will undergo temptation, but remember the promise of 2 Corinthians 10:13: "No temptation has overtaken you except such as is common to man; but God is faithful, who will not allow you to be tempted beyond what you are able, but with the temptation will also make the way of escape, that you may be able to bear it."

God has provided you with mighty spiritual weapons with which to combat the enemies you face (see Eph. 6:11-17), and the Holy Spirit within you is stronger than any force Satan sends against you. Therefore, "no weapon formed against you shall prosper" (Isa. 54:17). What happens if you fall? Don't stay down, because "if we confess our sins, He is faithful and just to forgive us our sins and to cleanse us from all unrighteousness" (1 John 1:9). Jesus gives you abundant, victorious life (John 10:10).

Continually renew your consecration with prayers such as this, taken from Romans 6:11-22):

"Lord Jesus, I consider myself dead to sin, but alive to God. Therefore, I will not let sin reign in my mortal body so that I will obey its evil desires. I present myself to God, as one who has been brought from death to life, and I offer the members of my body to You as instruments of righteousness. Sin shall not be my master, because the grace of God has freed me from its bondage. I am now a slave of Jesus Christ, and I have liberty, righteousness and eternal life."

I encourage each one of you to "grow in the grace and knowledge of our Lord and Savior Jesus Christ. To Him be the glory both now and forever. Amen" (2 Peter 3:18).